THE TWELVE

THE

12

A TRANSFORMATIONAL JOURNEY THROUGH THE MINOR PROPHETS

A COMPANION STUDY

PARKER BRADLEY

CONTENTS

INTRODUCTION

Welcome to this companion study to *The Twelve: A Transformational Journey Through The Minor Prophets*. In this seven-week study we'll consider several themes that are present in the twelve Minor Prophet's message to God's people in their day and also in our own.

While this study draws from the book The Twelve in how we navigate through the themes we discuss, you can easily enjoy this study without having read the book—though having your Bible handy is a necessity. At times we'll read parts of the Minor Prophets from our own Bibles. Short passages to be considered will be printed in the study itself.

Each week we'll consider something from three Minor Prophets (two in the group study version) as we explore the themes that they brought up most often. Sometimes we'll hear from a prophet more than once. As each prophet is introduced in the study, there will be a brief description of the prophet and the message God spoke through him. The book The Twelve goes into far greater detail into the time and message of each individual prophet. As you see a title in bold print in each section of the study, the content there will draw from ideas raised in the book, though much of this study is original in its content. Certain brief sections of the book are inserted where appropriate in this study as well.

As we go through each theme, the goal of this study is to help us unpack and understand the important message that God spoke to His people in the days of the prophets and how these timeless words speak powerfully to our own generation today. Let's allow these prophets into our lives and let their words draws us closer to Christ in order to be transformed by His grace into men and women of God who carry His light well into the world around us.

As I say in the book, the winds are always fair to set out on a new journey through the twelve Minor Prophets! I pray this study is encouraging and helpful for you.

Parker Bradley

GROUP STUDY

WEEK

ESSENTIAL
THE JUSTICE AND RIGHTEOUSNESS OF GOD

In today's world we may hear the word "justice" used in various places and situations. It might be a topic like social justice, racial justice, political justice, or a perceived injustice. And often, emotions and personal investment can run very high in matters attached to a sense of justice. The reason is simple: justice is vital in how we relate to one another and exist in community. Yet even worthy discussions and actions concerning justice can sink into hatred and resentment when a pursuit of justice is not accompanied by an equally strong measure of one thing—righteousness. In fact, without a good understanding of justice plus righteousness, that sense of justice can turn into tyranny very quickly no matter which side we may take. The best place to anchor oneself in any discussion about justice is in God's word where both justice and righteousness are not only defined, they are given their meaning and purpose in society as well as in the life of the church.

- What comes to your mind when we mention justice or righteousness?

- When have you heard topics linked with a sense of justice being brought up? Were the discussions intense, thoughtful, angry, helpful?

The prophets in Scripture weren't just interested in the justice and righteousness of God: they were completely preoccupied with them. And for good reason— these two are essential to the very character of God.

JUSTICE - (mishpat in Hebrew, sounds like "mish-pot")

When the term mishpat is used in the Old Testament, it typically means "judgment"- by God or in deciding a legal case and executing judgment according with the Law of God and His character.

Justice is a kind of <u>action</u> by a "judge." It is an act of judgment based upon a standard of what is to be considered right. The standard for justice in Scripture is set by God Himself.

MICAH c. mid 700s B.C

The Minor Prophet Micah wrote and prophesied around the same time as Isaiah near the end of the Northern Kingdom of Israel and at a critical time for the Southern Kingdom of Judah. The kingdom under Solomon split after his death (930 B.C.) due to some really poor leadership to become a Northern and Southern Kingdom with Jerusalem in the south. The Northern Kingdom promptly went off the rails and never recovered. Justice and righteousness went right out the window.

Look at how justice (or the lack of it) was referred to by Micah:

Hear this, you heads of the house of
   Jacob
  and rulers of the house of Israel,
who detest **justice**
  and make crooked all that is straight,
who build Zion with blood
  and Jerusalem with iniquity.
Its heads give **judgment** for a bribe;
  its priests teach for a price;
  its prophets practice divination for
    money.
Micah 3:9-11

● What seems to be making God angry in these verses
about justice?

RIGHTEOUSNESS - (tsedaqah in Hebrew, sounds like "zed-e-kah")

When the term tsedakah (or variant of it) is used in the Old
Testament, it refers to "a state of integrity in relation to God and
one's fellow man expressing itself in one's acts and speech."[1] It is a
guiding quality of true justice.

**Righteousness is more a <u>character quality</u> of the person making
the judgment. It is when one acts in conformity to what is
considered just by God's standard of justice.**

AMOS c. early to mid 700s B.C.

The Minor Prophet Amos is one you need to buckle up for when reading. God was speaking very directly to His own people who had perverted justice, cast righteousness to the side, and lived in whatever way they saw fit and beneficial no matter who was hurt in the process. God was not OK with that, especially when they pretended that everything was perfectly fine between them and God. They continued their regular worship services and religious services, singing their songs of praise to God while provoking Him to anger in how they ordered their lives in shameful ways.

Through Amos, God made His position very clear:

> I hate, I despise your feasts,
> and I take no delight in your solemn
> assemblies.
> Even though you offer me your burnt
> offerings and grain offerings,
> I will not accept them;
> and the peace offerings of your fattened
> animals,
> I will not look upon them.
> Take away from me the noise of your
> songs;
> to the melody of your harps I will not
> listen.
> But let justice roll down like waters,
> and **righteousness** like an ever-flow-

ing stream.

Amos 5:21-24

- Why was God looking for integrity from His people in how they lived, not just in how they maintained their religion? How are the two connected?

God's justice always acts in accordance with His own character and His <u>righteousness</u> as reflected in His <u>words</u> (including the Law and the Scriptures) and His <u>actions</u> (recorded in Scripture including sending Jesus to die for our sins).

The Major Prophet Isaiah had something to say about how God's justice and righteousness work together:

> And I will make justice the line,
>   and righteousness the plumb line.
Isaiah 28:17

Long ago, a builder would use a string with a weight on the bottom of it as a way to make sure that a wall or building was straight. By holding up the line with the weight at the bottom of it, a builder would **judge** whether the project was sound, secure, and solid. This verse states that "justice" is the line by which all things are measured. "Righteousness" is the weight that **holds justice in place** and keeps its judgments true. And what's more, these verses in Isaiah are ones that look forward to Jesus as the cornerstone and sure foundation! Justice and righteousness are the foundational measurements of Jesus' saving work.

- Righteousness holds justice in line. Why is that important?

THE QUALITY OF RIGHTEOUSNESS IS ALWAYS REFLECTED IN TRUE JUSTICE.

In the old Mosaic Covenant, an animal was sacrificed and its blood sprinkled on the altar as an atoning sacrifice to cover sins until the New Covenant came through Jesus Christ. Now, through the precious blood of Jesus, a lamb without blemish or defect, the righteous (Jesus) is given for the unrighteous (us) to bring us to God (1 Peter 1:19, 3:18). God's justice required the sacrifice of Christ to settle our sinful accounts, as it were. God Himself made the way for our forgiveness through Christ. He is just, demanding an accounting for sin. He is also righteous, compassionate, and merciful, sending his Son to be our sacrifice, dying once for all, to bring us back to Him. The justice and righteousness of God against wickedness and yet in compassion for those seeking Him in the Minor Prophets look forward to the cleansing work of the cross for you and me. Through Christ alone we are able to stand before God in that state of integrity we discussed earlier. Here's the proof—look at what God did for us through Christ and His cross:

> God made him who knew no sin to become sin for us that we might become the **righteousness** of God.
> (2 Corinthians 5:21)

Through the work of the cross, Jesus satisfied the **justice** of God on our sin so that by His redemption and reconciliation that is extended to all who believe, we can walk in that state of integrity having been made the very **righteousness** of God by faith in Jesus.

Let the weight of God's justice and the salvation in Christ through His righteousness and mercy move you to thankful prayer for His grace poured out on you in Christ. What a wonderful God He is!

CONCLUSION AND TAKEAWAYS

The justice and righteousness of God are major themes to consider and are found flowing throughout all of Scripture. As we read the Bible and seek to understand God's character and actions in human history, having a good grasp of justice and righteousness as God sees them is key. The good character of God in His righteousness always guides His justice.

- What are your takeaways from this study? What made the most impact for you?

- What are next steps God is leading you toward in walking through those things with Him? What may need to change for you? What conversations could you have with someone on this topic?

1. W Elwell and B. Beltzel, "Righteousness" Baker Encyclopedia of the Bible (Grand Rapids, MI: Baker Book House, 1988) 1860-1862.

WEEK

BEYOND LIP SERVICE
THE IMPORTANCE OF GENUINE FAITH

I t is unsettling at times to be asked to consider our motivations for something so cherished as worship on Sunday. The questions that these mighty Minors raise are not intended to make us feel like we're under a microscope. They are intended to call us to renewed faith and meaningful action. It's OK to let these prophets inside to look around. We'll be better for it!

A common theme in the Minor Prophets that isn't always fun to consider but is essential to a healthy Christian outlook and life is the theme of faith that isn't faked. That can feel like personal attack, but it isn't. God through these mighty prophets goes after self-pleasing religious expression with a vengeance. Why? Because of the great damage that can be done when what is at the core of who we are as believers is disingenuous. We might fool others and fool ourselves for a time, but when the rubber meets the road and times get tough, only a genuine faith in God that flows from the inside out will get us through. What God has to say through the Twelve doesn't drive dull religious drudgery; it fosters freedom and a faith that is prepared for every season of life. So let's allow these Minor Prophets in to look around and help us throw off what might hinder a vigorous vibrant faith.

GOD CALLS US TO A FAITH THAT IS NOT ONLY RIGHT–IT IS GENUINE.

HOSEA c.750-722 B.C

Hosea is one of the Minor Prophets that some may have heard of before because of his call by God to go and marry a prostitute in order to exemplify to God's people what it's like to be God to them. Unfaithfulness was the order of the day. God's message in Hosea is one from a broken heart earnestly calling out to a rebellious people. God was clear that such wickedness characterizing the ways of His people could not continue without His judgment, but He also called them back to Him with words of tenderness and love. Hosea's book is a torrent of emotion that highlights the love of our faithful God even for us who can be so unfaithful.

UH-HUH

But after all of the heartfelt expressions from a God who mercifully called His people back to Him with open arms, how did the people respond to His love and mercy? This one breaks your heart a little.

> Come, let us return to the Lord;
> for He has torn us, that He may heal us;
>   He has struck us down, and He will
>   bind us up.
> After two days He will revive us;

on the third day He will raise us up,
   that we may live before Him.
Let us know; let us press on to know
    the Lord;
  His going out is sure as the dawn;
He will come to us as the showers,
   as the spring rains that water the
    earth.

(Hosea 6:1-3)

The above poem or song would have been beautiful if it had been sincere from the beginning. In the chapters prior to this one, God turned His eyes to the priests who led His people astray. They were religious. They were polished. They knew how to talk "purdy," as we say in the South. How did God respond to this "gracious" and poetic outpouring?

What shall I do with you, O Ephraim?
  What shall I do with you, O Judah?
Your love is like a morning cloud,
  like the dew that goes quickly away.

(Hosea 6:4)

God said a big "uh-huh." If you're a frustrated parent, you may have said to your disobedient child, "What am I supposed to do with you?" as God did here. All of us know the feeling of being lied to, deceived, placated, or patronized. Doesn't feel good. We know that the people we're talking to think that if they say what we want to hear, we'll just go away. News flash: that doesn't work with God any more than it does with you. Even more so, He knows everything (1 John 3:20). After all the faithful and merciful outpouring of God upon this rebellious bunch, they responded by trying to tell God what they thought He wanted to hear so He would leave them alone and they could get back to business as usual.

- Why does it seem easier to tell people (and God) what we think they want to hear instead of speaking out of compassionate conviction or confession?

- What does it mean to you that we have a loving God who calls us back to Him even when we tend to be selfish and neglect our relationship with Him?

MALACHI c.440 B.C

The Minor Prophet Malachi was the last of the Biblical prophets to have a word from the Lord to share. After him, there was a very long silence until John the Baptist showed up saying to prepare the way of the Lord just before Jesus' ministry began. A major theme addressed in Malachi was seeking the favor of the powerful in government and the religious leadership to make life "better" instead of seeking God and His ways of fellowship and peace. Malachi likely spoke sometime around Nehemiah's time of rebuilding and beginning anew for Jerusalem. God's people needed renewed faith as well.

SHUT THE DOORS

We looked at how important genuine words and action are in our **relationship** with God. If there is one defining expression about how genuine we are in our relationship with God, it's in how we come to Him in **worship**. If we are less than genuine in our worship and praise of the God of our salvation, it's a good bet things aren't so great between God and us in daily life. Going through the motions doesn't work so well in a marriage. It also does not work well in walking with the Lord. So how important is genuine relationship and honest expression in worship to God? Listen to this:

> Oh that there were one among you who would shut the doors, that you might not kindle fire on my altar in vain! I have no pleasure in you, says the Lord of hosts, and I will not accept an offering from your hand.
>
> (Malachi 1:10)

God was saying here, "I wish that there were just one person in your religious leadership who was honest enough to recognize how fake and vain is what passes for worship that they would turn off the light and shut the door to this sanctuary." That is quite a statement.

God's good purposes for His people are ignored when we offer half-hearted worship and fool ourselves into thinking that merely performing some act of worship is what God desires.

 Read Malachi 2:5-8 in your Bible.

- What was God looking for from the religious leadership of the day? What was God calling out as harmful in their leadership of the people in His name? What harmful things might God call out in church leadership today?

- What does true worship from a sincere and repentant heart require from us? Why is it easy to let worship of God drift into a robotic and tiresome action?

CONCLUSION AND TAKEAWAYS

Walking in genuine faith with God is key to His blessing in our lives and our growth in Christ today. Trying to be clever and justifying our actions that keep hurting us (as well as others) is not the way to walk faithfully in the victory Christ has won over the brokenness of sin. Being genuine requires us to open up to God about every area of our lives and let Him work as only He can to make us into the men and women He means for us to be in Christ. It may not be easy work, but it's always good work that He does in us!

- What are your takeaways from this study? What made the most impact for you?

- What are next steps God is leading you toward in walking through those things with Him? What may need to change for you? What conversations could you have with someone on this topic?

WEEK 3 THIS IS UNCOMFORTABLE
ACCEPTING THE HARD WORDS OF GOD

The Minor Prophets often get a bad rap. Many think they are only full of wrath and judgment, lacking any love or hope for the future. Nothing could be further from the truth. If you really want to see the love of God on full display, outside of the Gospels, there is likely no better place than the Minor Prophets. Generation after generation God had called to His people to listen to Him and follow His ways of peace. He still does so in Christ to us today. The reason the Minor Prophets are so explicit is that God's people weren't listening. They were racing headlong into ruin. Sometimes God has to turn up His volume in order to get our attention. His strong words in these prophetic books do just that, but they are not words meant to wound. They are words meant to heal. The question is: are we listening?

WORDS THAT WOUND: WORDS THAT HEAL

Have you had those people in your life who have said things that you still carry around as scars? Maybe a coach, relative, or other authority figure? Maybe a friend who wasn't thinking? In any case, words can do more lasting damage to the mind and soul than just about anything. James 3 is pretty clear about that. The tongue can do a lot of damage to the soul. Words that wound for the sole purpose of wounding are bad. People may try to dominate, belittle, shame, or dismiss another person with wounding words. We all know what that's like. And, be honest, we have wounded intentionally with our words sometimes, too. **But can words wound with the intention of healing?**

Here's something to tuck away when you're reading the Bible. God's words to His people are ALWAYS meant to heal and bring us closer to Him. That includes the Minor Prophets. Healing words can be sweet and tender like many in the Psalms and the prayers of Paul. Healing words can also be difficult and even offensive at first. But God never wounds just to wound us. If He ever does wound with His words, it's because we probably won't listen to a nicer way because we're persistent in rebellion and selfishness of some kind. In short, we're hard headed. So take the tough words from God for what they are: healing words.

Look at these words from Hosea about the rebellious Northern Kingdom of Israel (Ephraim is the area where its capital was located):

> I know Ephraim,
>   and Israel is not hidden from me;
> for now, O Ephraim, you have played
>   the whore;
>   Israel is defiled.
> Their deeds do not permit them
>   to return to their God.
> For the spirit of whoredom is within
>   them,
>   and they know not the Lord.
>
> (Hosea 5:3-4)

Things had truly sunk to a low level for God to have to speak this way to His people. In business, politics, religious life, and in the community everything was "for sale." What guided their every move was what they could gain from the transaction and what should have been done for good was prostituted and perverted for personal gain. People were getting hurt in the process, and God's name was being dragged through that immoral mud. The reason for God's strong message here is revealed in verse 11 of the same chapter:

His people were "determined to go after filth." God knows where that road leads. He turned up the volume here to get His people's attention. **His words here were meant to wound but in order to encourage repentance and reconciliation.**

In these healing words spoken later in Hosea, look at what God wanted instead for His people:

> Sow for yourselves righteousness;
>   reap steadfast love;
>   break up your fallow ground,
> for it is the time to seek the Lord,
>   that he may come and rain righ-
>   teousness upon you.
>
> (Hosea 10:12)

God's hard words were meant to get His people's attention and call them to a reconciling work of blessing and steadfast love.

What God's people were doing was reaping just the opposite. God wanted to rain righteousness down upon His people and does today as well, but it requires that we leave ways of wickedness behind and pursue Christ instead. His strong words here still speak with the same shocking effect in a time where the battle over worldly cultural influence upon the church is very real.

- Why do you think people try to avoid the portions of Scripture that are more direct and straightforward about sin and its ill effects? Why might the Minor Prophets be seen as offensive to some?

- Do you remember a time when it was a hard word from God, your spouse, or from a true friend? What was it like to hear that word?

PREPARE

 Read Amos 4:4-13 in your Bible.

The book of Amos reveals the fierce love of God even for His wayward people. In Hosea, God said that He gave His people all of the things they needed, but they thanked their pagan gods for them instead. He gave and gave, but they would not return to Him. Now in Amos, God didn't bring blessings; He brought hardship and want. **God was clear: He was bringing the hardship upon them to get His people's attention.** However, the harder things became, the more His people turned away from Him. "Yet you did not return to me," God lamented repeatedly throughout Amos chapter 4. Whether times were good or times were bad, God was left out.

One of the most terrifying statements God made in the whole Bible comes up next. In the face of His own people's blatant rebellion, injustice, cruelty, perversity, and greed, God said He would personally bring the might of His wrath on this haughty nation in judgment. He said this in no uncertain terms:

> Therefore this will I do to you, O Israel,
>   because I will do this to you,
>   prepare to meet your God, O Israel."
> (Amos 4:12)

Those words were meant to drive people to their knees in prayer. Let me ask you this question that I have asked myself many times. Is this how God needs to speak to you to get your attention? Will you listen with a thankful heart as He sings songs of love and care over you? Or do you have to come up against the might of a just God because you keep burning it down in your sin and selfishness, dragging His name and yours through the mud? Come on, let's be real together. Are you hardheaded and stubborn in your sin? Always remember God's character: He wants us to return to Him in full confession and repentance so that He can pour out His blessings on us in peace. He is not mean and nasty. He is just. Who would want an unjust God except those who want a free pass to do whatever they feel like doing no matter what? People of conscience want a just God. But He is merciful, too. Only God can balance those two so perfectly.

How do you respond to the words of God in Amos? What do you conceive Him to be like? If there is something smothering your faith and crippling the abundant life you have in Christ, let Him reveal it. Don't dodge the hard words of God. Let them draw you to His side with greater speed and love than even His most tender words. Know His character. He works for your good through Christ our Lord, even in the furnace.

- Do the hard words of God make you want to come to Him or to run from Him? What do you think motivates those feelings? How does knowing God's character help us to see the goodness of God even His hard words?

- What we perceive God to be like is a huge predictor of how we respond and make choices in a given situation. How does having a high or low view of God play into how we might respond to the hard words of God?

CONCLUSION AND TAKEAWAYS

Walking in genuine faith with God is key to His blessing in our lives and our growth in Christ today. Trying to be clever and justifying our actions that keep hurting us (as well as others) is not the way to walk faithfully in the victory Christ has won over the brokenness of sin. Being genuine requires us to open up to God about every area of our lives and let Him work as only He can to make us into the men and women He means for us to be in Christ. It may not be easy work, but it's always good work the He does in us!

● What are your takeaways from this study? What made the most impact for you?

● What are next steps God is leading you toward in walking through those things with Him? What may need to change for you? What conversations could you have with someone on this topic?

WEEK

4 PERSPECTIVE
GOD'S WAY IS ALWAYS BETTER

From the very beginning with Adam and Eve right on through to our own day, the temptation to take over and be the one to call the shots is ever present. When that happens, what we are drawn to in an attempt to satisfy our fleshly desires takes a larger and larger role. It's not difficult to fall into a pattern of complacency and to let things build up into spiritual stumbling blocks. It's hard to run the race marked out for us in Christ Jesus (Hebrews 12:1) when we're tripping over ourselves half the time.

Happily, the Minor Prophets don't have a problem assisting us in noticing the junk that we can let pile up in our own lives. In fact, they are best friends to us in doing so because that sinful junk can ruin everything if we let it stay. Sometimes, the unhealthy patterns we create for ourselves can be very difficult to part with because we've become so used to them. Only our gracious God and loving Savior can walk with us through that process to find true freedom and victory in Jesus' name. Here, the Minor Prophets share words of truth and grace that come from the heart of God Himself to throw off what weighs us down. Then we can follow His paths of strength in freedom and right fellowship with Him.

LESSER GODS

ZEPHANIAH 640-610 B.C

Zephaniah spoke toward the end of the Southern Kingdom of Judah. His warnings were stern, and yet his statements about the enduring love of God are beautiful and timeless. His voice was among the last to be heard speaking God's words to His people before their rebellion brought His judgment with the fall of Jerusalem in 586 B.C. God was calling to His people yet again to turn from their ways marked by wickedness, corruption, and immorality and to return to Him who cared for them more than they could ever know. This mighty Minor speaks loudly to us today with the same sobering but hopeful message.

In my view, Zephaniah is dialed right in to a prevailing attitude in our modern world, at least in the West. Zephaniah stated it plainly enough:

> At that time…I will punish the men
> who are complacent,
>   those who say in their hearts,
> "The Lord will not do good,
>   nor will he do ill."
>
> (Zephaniah 1:12)

The imagery used here is interesting. The phrase translated "complacent" is literally "thickening on the dregs" in Hebrew. In making wine, the sediment (or dregs) had to be separated out from the wine itself or else it would thicken the wine making it undrinkable. **Leaving all the junk in there ruined everything in**

28

the process of developing a good wine. The junk had to go or else everything would be ruined—in winemaking as well as in life.

Those who "thickened on the dregs" in life just sat back and left the work half done. The corrosive impurities stayed. Why would they do that? Zephaniah hit the nail on the head: they said in their hearts that God was not going to do anything either way no matter what they chose. God was a nice idea but not a force to be reckoned with. "I can control my own destiny and don't need a God when I have myself and my self-sufficiency to worship. Lesser gods are fine with me, and I've made peace with whatever might offend God. I want to be left alone in my perceived security, thank you very much," is what this attitude may have sounded like.

- Have you seen this kind of complacent attitude today? Where? In your view how is that attitude expressed in words or actions?

2 Chronicles 33 related the moral and spiritual downfall of God's people in Jerusalem just before Zephaniah spoke. The Southern Kingdom had a horrible king named Manasseh along with his horrid son Amon. Kings, judges, scribes, and priests fell to all-time lows in perversity and wickedness under their leadership. They did what was right in their own eyes. Verse 10 summed it up: "The Lord spoke to Manasseh and to his people, but they paid no attention." Exactly. The leadership had a deal with the pagan nation of Assyria that cost them a lot, but they made it work by passing the price of tribute off on the people of God with taxes. The temple of God was decorated with the pagan images of Assyria and was eventually closed. Children were thrown alive into the fire in an attempt to appease these grotesque man-made gods by human sacrifice. What God desired and brought about for their good was cast aside in lust for power, money, pleasure, and security. "You can talk all you want, God, but this works for me. This feels right to me. This makes me money. I have international credibility. It might be messy for other

people, but whatever. The system works for me." They were fine with God as long as He kept His mouth shut on what they were doing.

Look at how God described this way of life in Zephaniah:

> Woe to her who is rebellious and defiled,
>   the oppressing city!
> She listens to no voice;
>   she accepts no correction.
> She does not trust the Lord;
>   she does not draw near to her God.
>   (Zephaniah 3:1-2)

- God called out "listening to no voice" and "accepting no correction." Why is that so dangerous? How do those actions lead to not trusting God and not drawing near to Him?

Being honest, we can tend to think very highly of ourselves and praise our own sense of justice and what should be morally acceptable in society and in religious life. We can do the "church thing" just fine without God or the Bible getting in the way. We can order our world and impose systems upon it that reflect our personal sense of what is good and just and fair—divorced from God. Any student of history can tell you how often mankind has tried that. Pride and arrogance fuel the selfish heart and always lead it to destruction, both on a personal level and on a national level. We desperately, entirely, and unquestionably need God to lead us every single day. It does not turn out well when we try to lead ourselves.

- Is it tempting in certain areas of your life to try and "lead yourself"? Which areas might you try and control more than others without listening to God first?

REND YOUR HEARTS AND NOT YOUR GARMENTS

To many today, being open and real means you say whatever comes to mind regardless of present company (preferably with some attitude). Today you need an aloof attitude towards sin and its effects, applauding any mode of self-expression because to not applaud would be judgmental. But in actuality, being open and real are the deadliest weapons to the sinful self. Those two expose everything. And that's good!

- Have you seen or experienced a time where being open and real from a Biblical point of view against modern morality has been deemed judgmental or hateful?

JOEL 800s - 700s B.C

Joel's message is one that is difficult for scholars to put a date on. He spoke about a great locust plague that had apparently just happened and devastated the land. He also spoke of a great human army that was on the way to wreak further havoc on God's people. Joel came to declare that those events were nothing less than God's judgment on His people over their sinful actions and repeated rejection of His ways of peace in the Law. The message was clear: stop doing those things and return to God and be spared His further judgment. Joel didn't list the offenses God's people were committing, but he did provide the way out—sincere and heartfelt repentance.

The below verses in Joel are the great doorway to the rest of his book. Here was where he got truly open and real. He didn't give us a list of offensive things that were being done at the time that incurred God's wrath. He only gave the remedy. **That meant that God was not only after a simple change in actions or outward appearance; the remedy went right to the heart.** Literally.

> "Yet even now," declares the Lord,
>   "return to me with all your heart,
> with fasting, with weeping, and with
>   mourning,
>   and rend your hearts and not your
>   garments."
> Return to the Lord your God,
>   for he is gracious and merciful,
> slow to anger, and abounding in
>   steadfast love,
> and he relents over disaster.
>
> (Joel 2:12-13)

What could have been going on in the culture that had carried God's people away from Him in their words, thoughts, and deeds? Joel doesn't really say. We may tend to get focused on what we are doing that's wrong—asking God all kinds of questions and psychoanalyzing everything. Questioning and trying to understand aren't wrong, but when they become our sole focus, to fix it ourselves or to figure it out, God gets left out. He's not the focus then; we are. God knows that, more than anything, we need the fountain of living water, His comforting and transforming Holy Spirit, filling the deepest parts of our hearts and souls. What we need is Him. "Return to me," He says.

It reminds me of what Jesus said in the Gospels:

> Come to me all you who labor and are heavy laden, and
> I will give you rest. Take my yoke upon you and learn
> from me, for I am gentle and humble in heart, and you

will find rest for your souls. For my yoke is easy, and my burden is light.

(Matthew 11:28-30)

Not "Come to a warped religious framework that you use to cloak your brokenness"; not "Come to a logical pattern of thought that makes sin less offensive and more palatable"; not "Come to a system that tells you everything is all right when it isn't." He said, "Come to me and I will give you rest." Our mighty Minor Joel reflected that call to come before God. Today we go to the person of Jesus in confession and repentance. Joel wasn't interested in games, fake faith, or pretty sounding words that didn't mean anything. Faith must be open and real.

- What qualities characterize a Christian life that is open and real in its expression and interaction with others?

The phrase Joel used in verse thirteen was only used once in the whole Bible, and it is powerful:

> return to me with all your heart,
> with fasting, with weeping, and with
> mourning,
> and rend your hearts and not your
> garments.
> (Joel 2:12-13)

Returning to God through the grace of Jesus after we've wandered away into the darkness has to be done with our whole heart. In fact, Joel says to tear our hearts over the confession of sin as they might have torn their robes in his day as an outward sign of grief. God is saying through Joel for our confession to be deep and from the heart, not just an outward superficial show. Have you had those times when you've come face-to-face with something you've done that you know broke God's heart? Perhaps you developed sinful patterns that consistently drew you away from God. Returning to God like the prodigal son did, falling on our knees and confessing the ruin we have created for ourselves is painful. It is also the doorway to forgiveness and freedom in Christ today. Joel said in 1:8 to lament like a virgin whose fiancé died tragically just before the day of their wedding. It is the recognition of great loss. Sin steals so much from us. Joel called the whole Jewish nation of his day to fasting, weeping, and mourning. That may not sound like much fun, but being open and real with God turns the hardened soil of a fallow heart and plants seeds of rich spiritual fruit that will last, nourishing everyone.

- Are there some sinful areas in your life that you haven't given to God? Are you hanging on to those thoughts, practices, and patterns? Don't feel judged—we all struggle with this at some point in our journey of being made more like Christ through faith. What keeps you from "being open and real" with God?

CONCLUSION AND TAKEAWAYS

There is true freedom for us in Christ in repentance from the "junk" we have allowed to stay in our patterns of living. Surrendering our will by turning from that junk in repentance and trusting in God's good will for us in Christ is the way to freedom and abundant life in Christ our Lord. Especially in those areas where we are most tempted to look elsewhere for fulfillment, blessing, and life, letting go of the sinful patterns and "junk" may be difficult, but Jesus brings healing and new life where darkness once ruled if we trust Him! God's way is always better.

- What are your big takeaways from this study? What ideas made the most impact for you?

- What do you think may be next steps God is leading you toward in walking through those things with Him in Christ? What may need to change for you? What conversations might you need to have with someone about these things?

WEEK

IDOL FACTORIES
THE TEMPTATION TO REDEFINE GOD

I dol worship may not be something we think about as a regular practice in our modern world. We may tend to think that idol worship may happen in less-developed countries and backward cultures. But from a Biblical point of view, idol worship is something that not only happens in modern culture and developed countries, it is a regular practice. Whenever we create things or turn to people to give us meaning, identity, purpose, prosperity, "the good life," or an attempt to acquire what we feel we lack as men and women, we become idol worshipers. Church reformer John Calvin (1509-1564 A.D.) made a bold admission of us as humans: he called us "idol factories."[1] And I hate to admit it, but he was right. It requires very little effort to become jealous, envious, lustful, greedy and led away by our sinful desires to become idol makers in our attempt to "complete" ourselves in our own way.

The theme of idolatry is repeated throughout the Minor Prophets because, just as in our own day, God's people were idol factories then as well. The messages of these books ring as true today as they ever did. And the outcome is the same—idols never bring what we desire of them. Setting our affections on the shiny distractions of worldly culture makes for an eye-catching but superficial façade that often hides a hurting and needy interior.

PRETTY CREATURES DO UGLY THINGS TO PEOPLE

At the end of God's last response to Habakkuk recorded in chapter two, God seemed to go off on a tangent. He had been decrying the pride and haughtiness of the Babylonians and offering woes and taunts that the nations under their domination would sing out once that nation fell. Then suddenly He shifted gears to talk about something that seems off topic—idolatry. It's not off topic at all. In fact idolatry is at the very center of the whole problem. Even today idols are everywhere. They don't have to look like a Babylonian god. They could look like a beautiful human body, wealth, status, or prosperity.

Anything that we put in God's place to bring us pleasure, fulfillment, blessing, or things desired apart from Him becomes an idol. They will bring you down into shame and ruin if you trust them.

Habakkuk shows us why.

Habakkuk mentioned the typical idols of his day: "a metal image," "a wooden thing," and "overlaid with gold and silver" (Habakkuk (2:18,19). **But what is most powerful about an idol is not its form or appearance but its influence, what it means to us, and what we look for in it.** The awful thing is that we project upon these idols ability and power that they do not and cannot posses. Habakkuk records:

> What profit is an idol
>   when its maker has shaped it,
>   a metal image, a teacher of lies?
> For its maker trusts in his own cre-

38

> ation
> when he makes speechless idols!
> (Habakkuk 2:18)

Today, we can certainly be led away to idols shaped by human hands and a sinful will. Worshiping idols can seem to feel right or even be enjoyable. It's the devastating aftermath that kills us with shame, grief, and disappointment along with the warped mental framework born out of bowing before idols. They poison our relationships. Idols, even beautiful ones, will never give you what you think you need from them. They deceive and keep you from God's bountiful blessing and peace—bringing instead your own hurt and destruction.

- Why do you think it is so tempting to look to something else or to someone else to bring us happiness, relief, or blessing instead of to God?

Here's the deal though: you and I both have been idol makers in our lives before. We made idols out of things that we looked to for blessing, prestige, relief, answers, and wealth apart from godliness. Idols are ugly things, and God speaks harshly against them through the whole Bible. Nothing replaces the goodness of an all wise, compassionate, teaching, and healing God. Nothing. That doesn't stop us from turning to things in our sin we would be ashamed for anyone to know about in search of the things only God can give. So what do we do, we idol makers?

First of all, repent of them. Smash those idols. If we have made people into idols, we should ask their forgiveness in tearful confession if possible. If we have made objects into idols, we must get a right perspective on the things God has given us for our good and relate to them without the lust that powers the idol maker. "So how do I do that? That seems like more than I can handle. I'm so used to living with my idols," you might say. And you'd be right. Only the mighty work of God through victorious faith in Jesus Christ can renew our minds and transform our hearts from idol factories into temples of praise to the One God who gives all good things to His beloved sons and daughters (James 1:17). Surrender your heart and mind to Him through Christ in confession and humility each day. He will make all things new. The difference between an idol and God Almighty is clear: idols lie and profit nothing because they are of our own making, weak and sinful as we are. Those who are on the side of truth and seek for it listen to Jesus, not idols (John 18:37).

God is not made by us. God's ways are "higher that our ways, and His thoughts are higher than our thoughts" (Isaiah 55:8-9). All that we need is found in Him through Christ our Redeemer. In His grace He reaches out to you and to me to abandon our idols and come near to Him through Christ to be filled as only He can fill us. The idols we create out of people and things may be very pretty and lovely in appearance, but pretty creatures do ugly things to people. Idols lie. God does not. Grind your idols into dust in repentance and confession before God. Let Him fill all things in every way. He will through Christ our hope.

- What are some idols you have been tempted to turn to in the past? How did God help you (maybe through a friend or an experience) turn away from that idol and to come to Him through faith in Christ?

WISHING GOD WERE DIFFERENT THAN HE IS

Sometimes it's not idols we create in attempts to shape the world around us to our liking; sometimes we may even try to twist God's words or to make God into someone He is not so we can feel more comfortable about the lives we desire to live. It's as though we try to make God into a "better God" according to our own personal judgments on the world and on other people. When we don't see people and the world around us in the same way that our redeeming and reconciling God does, emotions often get the better of us, and in our impatience, we may get frustrated with God and His ways that don't always agree with our feelings on how things should be.

As Jonah had to find out, God doesn't disregard our feelings, especially when difficult things have been suffered. Our Good Shepherd leads His dear children along on paths of righteousness that seek to bring healing to our hurts and hope and restoration to even the least deserving among us.

JONAH c.700s B.C

Jonah lived during a difficult time in Israel's history when the kingdom of Assyria was ravaging that part of the world with oppressive cruelty. God gave Jonah a message to deliver to those very people right in the heart of their capital city of Nineveh. Jonah, however, had other ideas and ran as far away from the call of God as he could. Even the possibility that the people who had inflicted such hardships on his people might be given the opportunity by God to repent was too much for him. Either they faced God's judgment and "got what was coming to them" or Jonah wanted no part of it. The story told in his amazing book is one of God's sovereignty over kings of the earth but also one of God's tenderness to a prophet who had a difficult time understanding that God's goodness extended to all who would hear His voice and repent.

What Jonah failed to see is that by the Assyrians' ceasing their evil ways of cruelty and oppression he and the people of Israel would be directly affected in measurably positive ways. The Ninevites' listening to God in this matter and acting in accordance with His peaceful design would also benefit everyone around them. But it didn't appear that Jonah could think that way at the moment. He saw only what had come before by their oppression and how hurtful it was. He wanted retribution. He wanted judgment for them for what they had done for so long. The message God gave him to deliver was, "Yet forty days and Nineveh shall be overthrown!" That was what Jonah was hoping for. That hits close to home. In today's deeply judgmental culture, we will dig through a person's past until we come up with something offensive and then demand they pay dearly for it whether or not we were affected by that past decision. We look to repayment of wrongs and the destruction of our offenders. What happens for you the day after all that judgment comes about for them? "I don't care!" we might scream. We want what Jonah wanted. We want the tables turned right now without any regard to the future. Peace tomorrow is not on the agenda. Retribution now is.

- Why is it so difficult to pray for and share God's love with those we deeply disagree with or may even have been wounded by somehow?

Leadership in Israel was at a low point, and God had to work through some real meatheads to bless His people at the time. When Jonah was alive, most likely Jeroboam II was king in Israel. Scripture states:

> [Jeroboam] restored the border of Israel from Lebo-Hamath as far as the Sea of the Arabah, according to the word of the Lord, the God of Israel, which He spoke by His servant Jonah the son of Amittai, the prophet, who was from Gath-

hepher. For the Lord saw that the affliction of Israel was
very bitter, for there was none left, bond or free, and there
was none to help Israel... so He saved them by the hand of
Jeroboam the son of Joash.

(2 Kings 14:25-27)

There it is. The people of Israel were "afflicted" and that affliction
was "very bitter." There was "none to help Israel." There just weren't
friends for Israel around at that time. No one wanted them there.
Not a fun time to be alive, especially for a prophet of God trying
to encourage his neighbors. If I try to place myself in that mindset,
the picture changes a bit. Jonah had no desire whatsoever for the
relenting of God's mighty justice on those wicked pagan people
in Nineveh. He was actually afraid of that peaceful outcome. He
lived in a time of very bitter affliction for his people. He wanted
judgment for those who were making life hard for them. In fact, he
made a stunning admission to that fact. He revealed his wounded
heart when he found out on the forty-first day that God would
honor Nineveh's grieving of their evil and changing of their ways—
God would relent. They would be spared His judgment. What
Jonah said to God in response to that mercy is shocking. He called
what God did, "evil" (Jonah 4:1).

- Have you personally experienced feeling that what God wanted
  in bringing about His will in a situation seemed wrong to you?
  Have you seen that in others as they seek out their desired view
  of life? How did God work out that situation?

We sometimes may want God to be different than He is because of
personal feelings that we have about a situation or experience. We
may even have very strong opinions on the matter. We might feel
like there are some who don't deserve mercy, as though we ourselves
do. Sometimes God is not easy to understand right off the bat.
However, God sees what we cannot. He knows what we do not. He

is above the tossing waves of a broken world, as Jesus demonstrated, though He is very present in it to redeem and restore. He sees beyond the hurtful present into a hopeful future found in Him. We have to trust Him. We know that "He works all things for the good of those who love Him and are called according to His purpose" (Romans 8:28). That doesn't mean that we see the whole picture like He does. Jonah needed an eternal perspective. I relate. It's hard not to be blinded by our own feelings, emotions, and experiences instead of letting God in Christ illuminate the true path that leads to peace with Him.

CONCLUSION AND TAKEAWAYS

As we've seen in spending time with the ol' Minor Prophets, being open and real is a must. The Twelve encourage us to not turn a blind eye to the things that keep tripping us up in our spiritual walk and certainly call attention to ungodly thinking that bears deceptive and malicious fruit in our lives. These Twelve might not be the guys you'd take to a party, but they just might save your life. Let's allow their words to guide our hearts toward Christ our Savior and Redeemer today.

- What are your big takeaways from this study? What ideas made the most impact for you?

- What do you think may be next steps that God is leading you toward in walking through those things with Him in Christ? What may need to change for you? How does this study spark ideas of conversations you might have with someone concerning God?

1. J. Calvin, "the human heart is a perpetual idol factory" Institutes (Louisville, KY: Westminster John Knox Press, 1960) 1.11.8

WEEK

WRECKED AND RESTORED
LIFTING OUR EYES ABOVE THE RUBBLE

I know for me, spending time with the Minor Prophets can shine a spotlight on areas in my life and spiritual walk with Christ that I don't often like to address. Those things I like to overlook are the very ones the Minors call to my attention. If we're not careful, we can miss the full message of restoration and redemption that comes from the Twelve. We might feel overwhelmed at the wreckage around us that we've tried so hard to live down or to which we may have surrendered in an attempt at peace.

God's message to us in the Minors is not to tear us down or to make us feel bad about our past choices. He means to clear the air and set forth a strong path forward with nothing hidden or making us stumble along the way as we follow Him in faith.

Over generations God's people had sunk into rebellion and corruption. God's ways were cast aside in favor of the ways of the world around them. The people of God had to endure the judgment of God in 586 B.C. when Jerusalem fell, the temple was destroyed, and God's people were carried into exile to a far away land. Looking around them at all the wreckage and ruin, they might have thought that there was no coming back from how far they had fallen and that God may have left them behind in their destruction with no hope of reconciliation.

We may have felt that way ourselves when having to come to terms with some choices we've made. The feeling of not knowing where to turn and that we have gone too far for God to forgive us may be a real feeling for many today. That's where our Minor Prophets shine the brightest.

God always makes a way in His mercy and grace where there seems to be no way to return to Him.

A WORD FOR THOSE WHO HAD LOST EVERYTHING

OBADIAH c.585 - 500 B.C

Obadiah spoke most likely in about 585 B.C after the fall of Jerusalem and the Southern Kingdom to the Babylonians, and he had the right thing to say at the right time to some deeply grieving people. Scholars disagree on when to date the book, but regardless of the date, the message was to encourage those who felt God had forgotten them. Obadiah spoke after a time of terrible conflict between God's people and their own neighbors, the people of Edom. What's worse is that the people of Edom were cousins to God's people, the Israelites. It was a family feud. A long and bitter hatred that was nurtured over generations resulted in the tragic cruelties that Obadiah was called to speak against. God showed through this mighty prophet that He was not only going to bring judgment against those who had acted in such cruelty against His people, He had not forgotten His once rebellious people and promised to lift them up and restore them to a marvelous kingdom of His own design.

Let's try to paint the picture. Imagine a spot in the center of ancient Jerusalem that is surrounded by rubble, filth, and charred beams that were once homes and marketplaces now lying in shattered bits all around. Smoke drifts about in the silent breeze rising from the smoldering piles that used to be a fabulous city capped off with a gleaming temple of white and bronze on the highest point. That temple is a ruin now, burned and broken. A lone dog barks in the distance, lost somewhere in an alleyway filled with wreckage. The remaining few people who survived the brutal attack by the most powerful army on earth stagger into the city center over the ruins, dodging the bodies trapped among the refuse. They say nothing. Some fall to the ground and weep. Hope is lost. God had poured out His wrath and abandoned them. . . or so they might think.

Then, from among the people rises a bearded and robed figure that raises his eyes above the rubble to the clear sky above. Lifting a hand he points his face in the direction of Edom and utters these words in full voice:

> Thus says the Lord God concerning Edom.
> (Obadiah 1)

The remainder of this short book speaks strongly against the awful things that had been done to God's people. God had not fallen silent. He had not forgotten His people, and He had seen all that had happened. He was rising up on behalf of His people. He is not aloof and distant in our hardship, even in the hardship we earned by our own actions. He is near if we will turn to Him in faith.

I know for me trying to look ahead at the good that can come out of a tough situation is not exactly easy. It's very natural to sit in a big stew of "bah humbugs" and misery. The cruelty and loveless action that happened in Obadiah's day by the people of Edom against the Judeans were not God's doing, but they did not happen without His knowing about it. The focus here shifted high above the rubble and far into the future. God said through Obadiah that things were about to change. The nations might not have known it yet, but God was up to something that included them as well. And His eye was on that very city that lay in ruins in Obadiah's day: Jerusalem. The temple would be rebuilt and serve as the anchor for God's people until the parables of His own Son echoed through its courtyards over 500 years later. Still, it may have seemed all but impossible for the people in Obadiah's day to see through their own tears. God's view is a longer view than our own. It's an eternal view. It's a Kingdom view. He is working on things we can't quite see yet. Through the prophets, He helps us see as He sees.

Obadiah is a reminder that God keeps His promises, that He does not reward evil, and that He is always about His greater Kingdom, now built on the cornerstone of Jesus Christ. Obadiah is part of God's greater redemptive story that is about restoring a right relationship with Him. That restoration is always done His way, not our way. His way is always better. He is faithful when we can be so faithless. He is a promise keeper when we can forget our promises and follow after things that hurt us. He is able to bring about His will no matter the situation. God knows how hard this world marred by sin can be. But He, in His goodness, does not forget those who are His by faith and call on His name in their distress and need. Lift your eyes above the rubble and smoke as Obadiah did. God is near through Christ His Son.

- Have you seen God redeem and restore an area of your life or maybe a broken relationship by His work in you through Jesus? If so, what was it?

THE WAY OUT

Without Hosea chapter 14, his book might be one of the saddest books we could read. But God does not lead us to the valley of the shadow of death; He leads us through it. Though the days may be difficult and hard to bear (especially if our own choices have led to the hardship we may be facing), when we finally open our wounded hearts up to God, He provides something desperately needed—a way out, a way to return to Him.

The very first word in Hosea's last chapter could be the one word that sums up the entire book. It's not an easy word, but did you expect an easy word from this mighty Minor Prophet? Best translated, the word is "Repent." The English Standard Version that I use says, "Return," but the idea is one of repentance—to stop going in the direction we're going and turn fully to God. I have found in my own life that repentance is the beginning of any significant transformation in Christ—certainly at the first confession of faith in Him, but also in times when we know we've strayed and need to return. We can't take the chains with us that separate us from Him when we do return. It doesn't work that way. We have to get real and "lay aside every weight and sin which clings so closely " (Hebrews 12:1).

- Why do you think it can seem easier to us to keep things status quo and live with our sinful patterns rather than take them to God to change us and lead us in new paths apart from those old patterns?

Look at these amazing verses:

> Return, O Israel, to the Lord your
> God,
>   for you have stumbled because of
>   your iniquity.
> Take with you words
>   and return to the Lord"
>
>   (Hosea 14:1-2).

I'm a little overwhelmed at the goodness of God here. He does not leave it up to us to find Him. It's not up to us to discover some secret door or do battle with the cosmos to return to God. He has done all the work and sets the path right before us. "Take with you words," He said. He even gives us the words to say, not as some magic charm or a rambling and repetitive mantra, but as a heartfelt prayer. In 1 John 1:9 we see this gift come to its fullest realization in Christ, that if we "confess our sins, He is faithful and just to forgive us and cleanse us of all unrighteousness." Look at what God asked here through Hosea:

> Say to Him,
>   'Take away all iniquity;
> accept what is good,
>   and we will pay with bulls
>   the vows of our lips.
> Assyria shall not save us,
>   We will not ride on horses
> And we will say no more, "Our God,"
>   To the work of our hands,
> For in you the orphan finds mercy.
>   (Hosea 14:2-3).

Hosea has his own style, so some of this wording is difficult. In short he is telling us to pray earnestly to God to do what only He can do: take away the stain and ugliness of our sin before Him. We are to ask God through Christ to accept the good and heartfelt prayer from our lips that is better than any religious sacrifice because we confess our utter dependence on Him. He said to confess that we have turned to powerful institutions and people to save us, or even worse, to our own might and self-reliance. We have made gods out of our own work and desired to control good and evil in our lives by our own strength and intelligence. We are truly as needy as orphans with no protector, and we plead for God's mercy. "Bring these words to me," God says, "and let me heal you." How beautiful. These words cut right to heart of our rebellion and selfishness. These words strip away the fake stuff and leave us bare before the God we have so deeply offended. But He gives us the words. He shows us the path. He lights the way out. Confess and return.

> I will heal their apostasy;
>   I will love them freely,
>   for my anger has turned from them.
> I will be like the dew to Israel,
>   he shall blossom like the lily;
>   he shall take root like the trees of
>   Lebanon;
>
> They shall return and dwell beneath my
>   shadow;
>   they shall flourish like the grain,
> they shall blossom like the vine.
>
> (Hosea 14:4-5,7)

This is the heart of God on display. "I will heal their apostasy; I will love them freely." Get real with God. Take with you words of deepest confession. Lay your sin and burdens down before Christ our Redeemer and Sustainer, God's Son, sent not to condemn the world but to save the world through Him (John 3:17). God is the faithful husband in Hosea's family picture. He loves you more deeply than you can fully know.

CONCLUSION AND TAKEAWAYS

There may be things in our past or even current trials that make us fearful of being open and real with God. But those things close us off from freedom in Christ and keep us trapped in patterns of thoughts and action that hurt us. God shows us the way out. That way is one where we have to leave those burdens behind that keep us from walking in close fellowship with Him and with our brothers and sisters in Christ.

In Christ today, we can lift our eyes from wreckage all around us and follow the good paths set forward by God through our mighty Minors who looked forward to Jesus' redeeming work and love beyond bounds poured out for us on His cross. Don't play with sin; repent of it. Freedom and peace are yours today through Jesus our living hope!

- What are your takeaways from this study? What made the most impact for you?

- What are next steps God is leading you toward in walking through those things with Him? What may need to change for you? What conversations could you have with someone about those thoughts?

7

WALK THE TALK
ACCEPTING THE HARD WORDS OF GOD

Well, we've made it to the final week! I hope you've enjoyed exploring some of the major themes in the Minor Prophets. Spending time with them forces us to ask tough questions of ourselves and be open and real with God about areas of our walk of faith in Christ that may need His cultivating work in order to better produce good fruit. It's always a good thing to come close to God and let Him work deeply within us, even if that process can feel like we're sitting in a furnace. "Uncomfortable" does not always equal "bad." Once the work is done and insights from it are gained, God raises us up to stronger faith in Christ by His Spirit to look without fear into the future and to stand boldly as beloved sons and daughters by faith. What can be said of our mighty Minors is this: when times were at their worst, these guys were at their best. No matter where we may be at present in our walk with Christ, time spent with the Minor Prophets is fruitful and encouraging.

WELCOMING THE FURNACE WORK OF GOD

James the Apostle knew something about the furnace of God and the good work He does there to prepare us for vibrant Christian life. In fact, James opened his New Testament letter with this statement:

> Count it all joy, my brothers, when you meet trials of various kinds, for you know that the testing of your faith produces

steadfastness. And let steadfastness have its full effect, that you may be perfect and complete, lacking nothing.
(James 1:2-4)

The phrase "testing of your faith" comes from the Greek word dokimos and relates to the firing process a pot must go through before it is ready for use. The clay is shaped by the potter and then placed into a blazing hot kiln to harden. In James' day, if that pot made it through the firing process without cracking, the word "dokimos" was written on the bottom of it by the potter. That was proof that this pot made it through the fire and didn't break up. It was ready for anything that it was required for. James was talking here about the kind of fire found in the furnace of God.

According to James, the end goal of God's furnace is steadfast faith in Him, full and lacking nothing. The furnace of God produces steadfast faith. That's why it's different: it has a purpose. Too many Christians, I believe, won't stay in the furnace when God turns up the heat to burn off the impurity and weakness within the vessel. Like "rend your hearts and not your garments" in Joel, the furnace of God can be a deeply painful place, especially for the prideful and rebellious. It gets too hot, and we hop out back into the lives we used to live that made us weak in our faith and impure in our minds. In doing so we render ourselves unfit for the greater use that was ours if we had stayed with God and let Him do His refining work.

Living like a Minor Prophet, as it were, can be summed up in three words: confidence in God. That means trusting confidently in God Almighty no matter what is going on in the world around us. There is nothing that the devil can throw at us to take away what God has given through faith in Christ: hope, determination of mission, and the life-giving knowledge that He will never leave us or forsake us but works all things for the good of those who love God and are called according to His purpose (Romans 8:28). It is One who walked upon the waves that we follow. What would threaten to take us out was no threat to Him. In Christ, we can walk in confidence knowing that though we may have trouble in this world, He has overcome the world. It is the tested faith that can boldly proclaim such things.

- Have you had a time when your faith was sorely tested? Are you in that time now? How did walking through that time with the Lord shape your faith? What can you share now with others that you could not share before that time?

- What is the most challenging part of yielding to God's work in your life? Do you sometimes close areas of your life off to God's good work?

I SHALL RISE

One of the biggest challenges in times of trial and hardship is keeping a right perspective. An eternal perspective is one that looks above the wreckage and rumbling going on around us to consider the ebb and flow of human activity according to God's ways and work in the world instead of our own limited view. It requires us to trust Him.

The last chapter of Micah is a real triumph of faith, but it began with Micah's looking around with his prophetic eyes to see the destruction that was coming because of the persistent sins of God's people. The Southern Kingdom had become completely unstable. The societal foundations were crumbling and the judgment of God was at hand. But Micah shifted his prophetic gaze in another direction and did so with a confident smile. He was not worried for himself or for the faithful remnant that would remain by God's grace. How is that possible in light of the judgment he knew was coming?

One word: relationship. Micah walked with God and knew Him through a personal relationship by faith. That changed everything. In the midst of it all knowing that he would have to live through the wrath of God that was coming on the land, Micah said:

> But as for me, I will look to the Lord;
>   I will wait for the God of my salvation;
>   my God will hear me.
>   (Micah 7:7)

Micah said plainly, "I'm not sure what you all are going to do when the bottom drops out and there is no place to hide, but as for me, I'm not seeing things the way you are. My eyes are not looking to the world around me. I will wait confidently for my God who will hear me and save me according to His steadfast love." Wow. Those three words: "I will wait." Without complete trust in God on every level, those words are hard. Micah's unshakable faith in the God of his salvation did not come by accident. It was not a disregard for reality or a pie-in-the-sky mentality that he had. It was a deep-seated confidence in the character of God because Micah knew His character through a personal walk with Him. That is the difference. The hope of Micah was not based on his own work or on the conditions of the world around him. He did not run from God when things got difficult before, and he won't run now—not because Micah was a great man. It's only because God is a great God who hears and saves. Micah's kind of hope comes through fire and faith, through testing and perseverance with God's help. Hope like that does not disappoint or put us to shame (Romans 5:5). Staring down the throat of tragic events to come that God revealed to Micah, our amazing prophet said boldly:

> Rejoice not over me, my enemy;
>   When I fall I shall rise;
>   When I sit in darkness,

The Lord will be a light to me.

(Micah 7:8)

Living like a Minor Prophet requires something else besides welcoming God's work in their lives: it requires God's higher *perspective.* Micah did not run from God in times of great trial. He ran to God. When what we have done shatters the foundations of our lives and family and when there is nowhere else to go but to God, we can still be tempted to run from Him. We can sense the ruin that is coming somehow and can stare right into the face of bitter consequence and still not bow the knee in confessing our brokenness before God. "I will bear it," says Micah, because in God's transforming grace, "When I fall I shall rise." He trusted in God to raise him up.

- Has there been a time in your life when you didn't know who to trust and you felt that if you shared your heart on a matter that people might be hostile to your deeply held belief? How did you respond in that situation?

- What is the hardest part of trusting God in fearful times or in times where the outcome is unclear at the moment? How does trusting in God's character help you to look at the future differently? What part of His character do you cling to most?

CONCLUSION AND TAKEAWAYS

Welcoming God's work in our lives, maintaining a God-given perspective by faith, and leaning on the truth that God is with us who trust in Christ His Son are three major themes that can give us the confidence in God that the Minor Prophets had during the difficult days that they faced.

- What are your takeaways from this study? What made the most impact for you?

- What are next steps God is leading you toward in walking with more confident faith in Him? What may need to change for you? What conversations could you have with someone struggling with trusting God?

SELF-GUIDED STUDY

ESSENTIAL
THE JUSTICE AND RIGHTEOUSNESS OF GOD

L et's jump right into the deep end of the pool and talk about two of the most important themes not only of the Minor Prophets but also the Bible itself. If we begin with a good understanding of the justice and righteousness of God, the beauty of the Minor Prophets will shine out all the brighter and give comfort, strength, and hope in every situation.

In today's world we may hear the word "justice" used in various places and situations. It might be a topic like social justice, racial justice, political justice, or a perceived injustice. And often, emotions and personal investment can run very high in matters attached to a sense of justice. The reason is simple: justice is vital in how we relate to one another and exist in community. Yet even worthy discussions and actions concerning justice can sink into hatred and resentment when a pursuit of justice is not accompanied by an equally strong measure of one thing—righteousness. In fact, without a good understanding of justice plus righteousness, that sense of justice can turn into tyranny very quickly no matter which side we may take. The best place to anchor oneself in any discussion about justice is in God's word where both justice and righteousness are not only defined, they are given their meaning and purpose in society as well as in the life of the church.

The justice and righteousness of God are monumental themes that pervade the whole Bible, especially the message of the Minor Prophets.

WHY START HERE?

Justice that is impartial and a compassion that fuels that justice are primary. A well-guided sense of right and wrong are necessary for making everyday decisions in life as well as for good governance, strong church life, and being good neighbors. Neglect or rejection of rightly guided justice in favor of an intended outcome always messes things up for us and for those around us. Injustice always tears down. Christian author C.S. Lewis shed light on this issue well when he stated:

> If you leave out justice you will find yourself breaking agreements and faking evidence in trials 'for the sake of humanity,' and become in the end a cruel and treacherous man.[1]

(Lewis, *Mere Christianity*)

The stakes are as high today as they were in the days of the Minor Prophets in the question of justice and righteousness. God spoke to all aspects of society in addressing the injustice that He saw from His own people as well as from the world around them. The ground that the Minor Prophets covered was immense, and their words left no one untouched:

FROM THE TWELVE

The situation in each Minor Prophet's day had reached a tipping point, and God needed to warn those who would hear Him of what was coming if things didn't change. These prophets spoke to their own neighbors and to the heights of power. They spoke to people who claimed to know God and to those who cared little about Him. They spoke to the poor and downtrodden and to some of the most powerful nations in world history. They spoke to gentle souls who loved God and loved people, and they spoke to violent oppressors who cast God to the side and destroyed whole groups of people through human atrocities I hope we can't imagine.

(page 8)

These prophets wasted no words and cut right to the heart of the issue. Their books resonate just as powerfully now as they ever did.

Even today the justice and righteousness that God requires is not only to be found among fellow believers in Christ. He judges the whole of humanity against it as Sovereign Lord of the world He has made. In short, it's hard to make too big of a deal of justice and righteousness when considering the ways of God and His character as revealed in Scripture.

- What comes to your mind in when we mention justice or righteousness?

- When have you heard topics linked with a sense of justice being brought up? Were the discussions intense, thoughtful, angry, helpful?

COMING TO TERMS

We may have a general concept of justice if someone were to press us to define it. We may not have as firm an idea of what righteousness is. And as we're about to see, righteousness is the more important of the two! Righteousness informs justice and not the other way around.

So that we don't get too broad in our discussion, let's narrow down a bit. The first thing we should do is to define justice and righteousness from a biblical perspective (and even learn a little Hebrew as well!).

JUSTICE – (MISHPAT IN HEBREW, SOUNDS LIKE "MISH-POT")

When the term *mishpat* is used in the Old Testament, it typically means "judgment"- by God or in deciding a legal case and executing judgment according with the Law of God and His character.

Justice is a kind of <u>action</u> by a "judge." It is an act of judgment based upon a standard of what is to be considered right. The standard for justice in Scripture is set by God Himself.

MICAH c. mid 700s B.C

The Minor Prophet Micah wrote and prophesied around the same time as Isaiah near the end of the Northern Kingdom of Israel and at a critical time for the Southern Kingdom of Judah. The kingdom under Solomon split after his death (930 B.C.) due to some really poor leadership to become a Northern and Southern Kingdom with Jerusalem in the south. The Northern Kingdom

promptly went off the rails and never recovered. Justice and righteousness went right out the window.

Look at how justice was referred to by Micah:

> Hear this, you heads of the house of
>   Jacob
>   and rulers of the house of Israel,
> who detest **justice**
>   and make crooked all that is straight,
> who build Zion with blood
>   and Jerusalem with iniquity.
> Its heads give **judgment** for a bribe;
>   its priests teach for a price;
>   its prophets practice divination for
>   money.
>
> (Micah 3:9-11)

● What seems to be making God angry in these verses about justice?

RIGHTEOUSNESS - (TSEDAQAH IN HEBREW, SOUNDS LIKE "ZED-E-KAH")

When the term *tsedakah* (or variant of it) is used in the Old Testament, it refers to "a state of integrity in relation to God and one's fellow man expressing itself in one's acts and speech."[2] It is a guiding quality of true justice.

Righteousness is more a <u>character quality</u> of the person making the judgment. It is when one acts in conformity to what is considered just by God's standard of justice.

In business, government, church leadership, and in community with others, that state of integrity according to God's compassionate and merciful ways must guide what we say and do. But how can we ever achieve a state of integrity before God Almighty so that we can live that kind of life before Him? Hang on to that question for a bit. The answer is a major one. First, let's look at righteousness a little more closely.

AMOS c. early to mid 700s B.C.

The Minor Prophet Amos is one you need to buckle up for when reading. God was speaking very directly to His own people who had perverted justice, cast righteousness to the side, and lived in whatever way they saw fit and beneficial no matter who was hurt in the process. God was not OK with that, especially when they pretended that everything was perfectly fine between them and God. They continued their regular worship services and religious services, singing their songs of praise to God while provoking Him to anger in how they ordered their lives in shameful ways.

Through Amos, God made His position very clear:

> I hate, I despise your feasts,
>   and I take no delight in your solemn
>   assemblies.
> Even though you offer me your burnt
>   offerings and grain offerings,
>   I will not accept them;

and the peace offerings of your fattened
   animals,
   I will not look upon them.
Take away from me the noise of your
   songs;
   to the melody of your harps I will not
   listen.
But let justice roll down like waters,
   and **righteousness** like an ever-flowing stream.
(Amos 5:21-24)

● Why was God looking for integrity from His people in how
  they lived, not just in how they maintained their religion? How
  are the two connected?

Jewish scholar and author Abraham Joshua Heschel detailed justice
and righteousness in his influential book found on many pastors'
shelves, *The Prophets*. In unpacking these terms, he made this clear
observation:

   Righteousness goes beyond justice. Justice is strict and
   exact, giving each person his due. Righteousness implies
   benevolence, kindness, generosity. Justice may be legal;

righteousness is associated with a burning compassion for the oppressed.[3]

(Heschel, *The Prophets*)

Here's the part where God's justice and human justice may part at times. Justice as defined by God is *utterly dependent* upon righteousness (benevolent, kind, generous according to God's character). The judgment given by the "judge" must be righteous in its makeup. Any act of justice that is not foundationally righteous can easily become an act of *in*justice, no matter its intention. In speaking with a friend of mine on this subject matter, he got right to the difficulty some might have with pursuing justice. He commented, "Justice in the smaller sense (between people) can be sought and argued over, but to me it almost always involves opinion and personal bias. We want justice when we have been wronged or see a particular wrong we want righted, but never want justice when we are the wrongdoer or the guilty party."[4] That hit the target. For justice to be just, it must be based on something higher than personal opinion, perspective, or feeling.

So what defines true justice, God's justice? Let's look.

God's justice always acts in accordance with His own character, His righteousness as reflected in His words (including the Law and the Scriptures) and His actions (recorded in Scripture including sending Jesus to die for our sins).

Consider this telling verse from Isaiah that Dr. Heschel pointed out:

> And I will make justice the line,
>   and righteousness the plumb line.
> > (Isaiah 28:17)

Long ago, a builder would use a string with a weight on the bottom of it as a way to make sure that a wall or building was straight. By holding up the line with the weight at the bottom of it, a builder

70

would **judge** whether the project was sound, secure, and solid. This verse states that "justice" is the line by which all things are measured. "Righteousness" is the weight that holds justice in place and keeps its judgments true. And what's more, these verses in Isaiah are ones that look forward to Jesus as the cornerstone and sure foundation! Justice and righteousness are the foundational measurements of Jesus' saving work.

- Righteousness holds justice in line. Why is that important?

- If God's justice is strict and exact, why is it important that His burning compassion for the oppressed guide His justice?

Dr. Heschel made this important observation:

> The word *mishpat* (justice) means the judgment given by the *shofet* (judge). While legality and *tsedekah* (righteousness)

are not identical, they must always coincide, the second being reflected in the first.[5]

(Heschel, *The Prophets*)

THE QUALITY OF RIGHTEOUSNESS IS ALWAYS REFLECTED IN TRUE JUSTICE.

God's justice (and even His wrath) is never separated from His burning compassion for the oppressed. His goodness and His justice are not at odds. Again, righteousness holds justice in line. That may be hard to grasp for some. The wrath of God is an idea that is uncomfortable to consider. How could His wrath and His compassion coexist? Our Minor Prophets lead the way on this point.

- Describe what justice without righteousness might look like. Why is it important to God that justice be guided by righteousness?

The prophets in Scripture weren't just interested in the justice and righteousness of God: they were completely preoccupied with

them. And for good reason— these two are essential to the very character of God.

An important point to remember about God's true justice is that it is about that very thing—justice. God's justice doesn't work merely to destroy those who disagree or simply to inflict punishment on the offender. **He first calls for repentance so that the wayward might return to Him or to ways that are in line with His righteousness. He called out through His prophets in the Old Testament so that judgment might be** *avoided.* However, though slow to anger and abounding in love, once God acts in judgment on the wickedness of sin, there is no escaping it. Let's look at Nahum's message and how the cross of Christ casts a long shadow into the Minor Prophets when it comes to the wrath of God on the sinfulness of humanity.

NAHUM c. 620s B.C.

The Minor Prophet Nahum spoke at a difficult time in the history of God's people. The neighboring pagan kingdom (Assyria) that the Northern Kingdom sought to emulate instead was the one that utterly destroyed it in the end (722 B.C.). God's people may have wondered if God would ever rise up to rescue them from such calamity and hardship, especially after all they had done to offend and reject Him. Nahum reminds God's downcast people then and now of God's character and that He will always act in accordance with it. Though it might sound pretty stormy to us, this book would have been music to the ears of anyone in that day that feared for their lives under the oppressive rule of cruel Assyria with its capital of Nineveh.

If there's one place to consider the justice and righteousness of God, it's here in this powerful book.

Earlier in Jonah's day (c. early 8th century), the Assyrians (with Nineveh as their capital) had ceased their military conquests and oppressive practices. God sent Jonah to that very city to warn them of His judgment if their cruelties did not stop. Their repentance did not last very long, however. A brutal leader named Tiglath-pileser III rose to power in the Assyrian kingdom (745-727 B.C.) and quickly began to subdue the peoples of the near east with violent fury inflicting horrific atrocities on captives or exacting crippling tribute. Other Assyrian kings followed suit. Proud of their exploits in battle, the Assyrians preserved these acts in their art. Stone-carved reliefs from near this time can be seen in the British Museum today. Nahum 1:14 is one of the most disturbing verses one could read: "I will make your grave for you are vile." For God to say He is personally digging your grave, something had to have gone terribly wrong. God was not allowing that evil to continue. The very last verse of Nahum reveals what motivated God to act on behalf of the people of the land: "For upon whom has not come your unceasing evil?" (Nahum 3:19). God's words were great comfort to those who suffered under Assyrian tyranny. They were no comfort at all for the oppressive capital city of Nineveh and those within her who thought themselves too powerful to be reckoned with and too mighty to be humbled.

Did God's justice guided by His righteousness rise up in defense of those suffering mightily under the bloodthirsty violence and subjugation of Nineveh? Yes it did. God's burning compassion guides His just acts against Assyria's cruelty. Nahum is filled with unrelenting woe and declarations of doom for those who stood for the injustices being committed and human atrocities being carried out in pursuit of domination of those around them. God is a God of justice who always acts in accordance with His character. He is the God any lover of true justice will run to.

- What might you talk about with someone you know who is very active in a social justice movement of some kind?

 Read Nahum 1:1-7 in your Bible.

That's quite an introduction!

- What are some words or phrases that stick out to you in this passage? How is God described here?

So that we don't misunderstand what God is saying, let's look deeper and put things in better focus. This opening passage actually looks back to a much earlier time when God revealed His character to His people in the book of Exodus many centuries before. That God is a jealous God (meaning zealous, deeply concerned, and watchful) comes from Exodus 20:5 as He gave the Ten Commandments. These words reminded the hearers that God was not distant from what they were experiencing. He knows what is going on and is deeply concerned and watchful over His people. He will act on His people's behalf. That is also a comfort to us today as followers of Christ.

Nahum 1:3 declared that God is "slow to anger, great in power, and by no means clears the guilty" which comes from a very famous and often quoted passage in Exodus 34. There God declared His character to Moses on the mountain. References to these defining verses are found all over the Bible. It's clear God wants us to know His character.

 Read Exodus 34:6-7 in your Bible.

● What are some words and phrases God used to describe His eternal character?

Because of the situation in his day, Nahum zeroed in on the last portion of God's declaration—*He by no means clears the guilty.* That sounds harsh, and it is meant to sound harsh, especially in the face of brutal injustice. That statement speaks to something essential about God: He is just. He doesn't turn a blind eye to the awful things we can do to one another nor does He sweep sin under the rug. The brokenness of sin and the wounding hurtful actions that arise from it are things a just God must address. American pastor Adrian Rogers said, "When a guilty man is acquitted, the judge is condemned."[6] A judge must execute true justice. That is his role.

What the Exodus passage reveals is not that God is on the side of justice or that He desires justice; it reveals that God is just. It is essential to His character. He cannot be unjust. He acquits no guilty man or woman. But we are all guilty of sin and deserving of judgment, you might say! And you'd be right! God's justice never sweeps sin under the rug. He demands it be answered. Remember, He is just. But in His compassion, He is also righteous: He provides a way for our guilt to be fully addressed in His kindness and mercy.

In the old Mosaic Covenant, an animal was sacrificed and its blood sprinkled on the altar as an atoning sacrifice to cover sins until the New Covenant came through Jesus Christ. Now, through the precious blood of Jesus, a lamb without blemish or defect, the righteous (Jesus) is given for the unrighteous (us) to bring us to God (1 Peter 1:19, 3:18). God's justice **required** the sacrifice of Christ to settle our sinful accounts, as it were. God Himself made the way for our forgiveness through Christ. **He is just, demanding an accounting for sin. He is also righteous, compassionate, and merciful, sending his Son to be our sacrifice, dying once for all, to bring us back to Him.** The justice and righteousness of God against wickedness and in compassion for those seeking Him in Nahum look forward to the cleansing work of the cross for you and me. Through Christ alone we are able to stand before God in that state of integrity we discussed earlier. Here's the proof—look at what God did for us through Christ and His cross:

> God made him who knew no sin to become sin for us that we might become the **righteousness** of God.
>
> (2 Corinthians 5:21)

Through the work of the cross, Jesus satisfied the **justice** of God on our sin so that by His redemption and reconciliation that is extended to all who believe, we can walk in that state of integrity having been made the very **righteousness** of God by faith in Jesus.

While Nahum does not mention the crucifixion or Jesus the Messiah directly, his strong message of the justice of God leads straight to the cross where justice, righteousness, and mercy met perfectly in the sacrificial death of Christ on our behalf. The justice of God is something the Assyrians of Nineveh saw up close, and with no repentance this time, they were crushed by a God who by no means clears the guilty. You and I and every living soul as errant sinners come up against that same justice of God. This should inspire some fear. But hallelujah, Christ Jesus became the sacrifice that satisfied the justice of God, who in His righteous mercy sent His only Son to save and redeem the lost. This should inspire some excitement and deep thankfulness from born again sons and daughters of God and everyone who seeks God's forgiveness through Jesus!

- As you consider the justice and righteousness of God, how are they reflected in Jesus' death and resurrection?

Nahum is not an easy prophet to read, but when we remember that it is a just God guided by burning compassion and care for those whose are hurting, the tone of the book opens up to reveal the comfort this book gave to the original hearers suffering as they did under this wicked kingdom.

Followers of Christ today can take great comfort in the verse that seems to come out of the blue in Nahum 1:7:

> The Lord is good,
>   A stronghold in the day of trouble;
> He knows those who take refuge in him.
>   (Nahum 1:7)

At the very beginning of this stormy book, we plant our feet firmly on the character of God. He is good. He is a stronghold in difficult times for those who run to Him. He knows those who call on Him personally and is watchful, zealous, and deeply concerned for them. Go ahead and spend time with this amazing Minor Prophet resting your soul in the justice and righteousness of God. Let the weight of God's justice and the salvation in Christ through His righteousness and mercy move you to thankful prayer. What a wonderful God He is!

CONCLUSION AND TAKEAWAYS

The justice and righteousness of God are major themes to consider and are found flowing throughout all of Scripture. As we read the Bible and seek to understand God's character and actions in human history, having a good grasp of justice and righteousness as God sees them is key. The good character of God in His righteousness always guides His justice.

- What are your takeaways from this study? What made the most impact for you?

- What do you think may be next steps God is leading you toward in walking through those things with Him in Christ? What may need to change for you? What conversations could you have with someone on this topic?

BEYOND LIP SERVICE
THE IMPORTANCE OF GENUINE FAITH

WEEK

2

I t is unsettling at times to be asked to consider our motivations for something so cherished as worship on Sunday. The questions that these mighty Minors raise are not intended to make us feel like we're under a microscope. They are intended to call us to renewed faith and meaningful action. It's OK to let these prophets inside to look around. We'll be better for it!

GOD CALLS US TO A FAITH THAT IS NOT ONLY RIGHT—IT IS GENUINE.

A common theme in the Minor Prophets that isn't always fun to consider but is essential to a healthy Christian outlook and life is the theme of **faith that isn't faked**. That can feel like personal attack, but it isn't. God through these mighty prophets goes after self-pleasing religious expression with a vengeance. Why? Because of the great damage that can be done when what is at the core of who we are as believers is disingenuous. We might fool others and fool ourselves for a time, but when the rubber meets the road and times get tough, only a genuine faith in God that flows from the inside out will get us through. What God has to say through the Twelve doesn't drive dull religious drudgery; it fosters freedom and a faith that is prepared for every season of life. So let's allow these

Minor Prophets to help us throw off what might hinder a vigorous vibrant faith.

UH HUH

Have you said that before to someone you thought was being less than genuine? Or maybe they were totally trying to snow you and you could see right through it? Have you had someone say it to *you* because you were trying to snow *them*? Their eyes narrow and they crane their neck back a bit, drop their tone and say it: "Uh huh." Let's be honest, sometimes we think we can talk our way out of anything. What we say and what we do need to match up.

HOSEA c.750-722 B.C

Hosea is one of the Minor Prophets that some may have heard of before because of his call by God to go and marry a prostitute in order to exemplify to God's people what it's like to be God to them. Unfaithfulness was the order of the day. God's message in Hosea is one from a broken heart earnestly calling out to a rebellious people. God was clear that such wickedness characterizing the ways of His people could not continue without His judgment, but He also called them back to Him with words of tenderness and love. Hosea's book is a torrent of emotion that highlights the love of our faithful God even for us who can be so unfaithful.

But after all of the heartfelt expressions from a God who mercifully called His people back to Him with open arms, how did the people respond to His love and mercy? This one breaks your heart a little.

> Come, let us return to the Lord;
> for He has torn us, that He may heal us;
>   He has struck us down, and He will
>   bind us up.
> After two days He will revive us;
>   on the third day He will raise us up,
>   that we may live before Him.
> Let us know; let us press on to know
>   the Lord;
>   His going out is sure as the dawn;
> He will come to us as the showers,
>   as the spring rains that water the
>   earth.
>
> (Hosea 6:1-3)

The above poem or song would have been beautiful if it had been sincere from the beginning. In the chapters prior to this one, God turned His eyes to the priests who led His people astray. They were religious. They were polished. They knew how to talk "purdy," as we say in the South. How did God respond to this "gracious" and poetic outpouring?

> What shall I do with you, O Ephraim?
>   What shall I do with you, O Judah?
> Your love is like a morning cloud,
>   like the dew that goes quickly away.
>
> (Hosea 6:4)

God said a big "uh-huh." If you're a frustrated parent, you may have said to your disobedient child, "What am I supposed to do with you?" as God did here. All of us know the feeling of being lied to, deceived, placated, or patronized. Doesn't feel good. We know that the people we're talking to think we're somehow stupid and that if they say what we want to hear, we'll just go away. News flash:

83

that doesn't work with God any more than it does with you. Even more so, He knows everything (1 John 3:20). After all the faithful and merciful outpouring of God upon this rebellious bunch, they responded by trying to tell God what they thought He wanted to hear so He would leave them alone and they could get back to business as usual. How do you think God responded through Hosea? Read this:

> Therefore I have hewn them by the
> prophets;
> I have slain them by the words of my mouth,
> and my judgment goes forth as the
> light.
> For I desire steadfast love and not
> sacrifice,
> the knowledge of God rather than
> burnt offerings.
>
> But like Adam they transgressed the
> covenant;
> There they dealt faithlessly with me.
>
> For they sow the wind,
> and they shall reap the whirlwind.
> (Hosea 6:5-7, 8:7)

God knows what sin does to us. He hates it. His words are strong. The relationship that He made you to be in with Him is not possible if you deceive Him with empty worship so you can get back to sin as usual.

God is telling us what we don't want to hear. He sees through our patronizing words and hews us like planks of wood and slays us with the words of His mouth in order to wake us up and to shake us out of a droning religious slumber.

God desires **steadfast** love. That is love that won't leave. He knows what is coming if we wander away and persist in sin. It is terrible. "They sow the wind, and they shall reap the whirlwind." We think we can handle a small breeze, as sin may appear at the beginning. But what is sown grows and grows. No one can handle a tornado. A little bit of sin goes a long way. That occasional porn usage, that flirting with the married coworker, that burning jealous hate, that selfish ambition to overpower in underhanded ways—they seem small at the beginning. You may have a personal testimony of what began as a breeze that became a tornado that wrecked everything. **God knows what sin can do to us. That's why His words are strong sometimes in the Minor Prophets.**

Let's be honest with God and with each other. Hosea is an in-your-face kind of guy, but God is directing this prophet's words to bring you and me home now in Christ Jesus in genuine, steadfast love.

- Why does it seem easier to tell people (and God) what we think they want to hear instead of speaking out of compassionate conviction or confession?

- What does it mean to you that we have a loving God who calls us back to Him if we wander away into hurtful places?

SHUT THE DOORS

We looked at how important genuine words and action are in our **relationship** with God. If there is one defining expression about how genuine we are in our relationship with God, it's in how we come to Him in **worship**.

MALACHI c.440 B.C

The Minor Prophet Malachi was the last of the Biblical prophets to have a word from the Lord to share. After him, there was a very long silence until John the Baptist showed up saying to prepare the way of the Lord just before Jesus' ministry began. A major theme addressed in Malachi was of seeking the favor of the powerful in government and the religious leadership to make life "better" instead of seeking God and His ways of fellowship and peace. Malachi likely spoke sometime around Nehemiah's time of rebuilding and beginning anew. God's people needed a renewed faith as well.

If we are less than genuine in our worship and praise of the God of our salvation, it's a good bet things aren't so great between God and us in daily life. Going through the motions doesn't work so well in a marriage. It also does not work well in walking with the Lord. So how important is genuine relationship and honest expression in worship to God? Listen to this:

> Oh that there were one among you who would shut the doors, that you might not kindle fire on my altar in vain! I

have no pleasure in you, says the Lord of hosts, and I will not accept an offering from your hand.

(Malachi 1:10)

God was saying here, "I wish that there were just one person in your religious leadership who was honest enough to recognize how fake and vain is what passes for worship that they would turn off the light and shut the door to this sanctuary." That is quite a statement.

God's good purposes for His people are ignored when we offer half-hearted worship and fool ourselves into thinking that merely performing some act of worship is what God desires.

Abundant life in Christ cannot take root in soil that also fosters vanity. Sadly, this wasn't the first time God had to address questionable motivations from His people in their religious duties and worship of Him. Robotic worship that should be filled with thanksgiving and praise reveals a lot about the state of the person uttering it and what they think of God. It offends God deeply when a time that should be celebrating our relationship with Him through Christ becomes a heartless chore.

Jesus also had something to say on this personal subject. To the Jewish religious leaders who were caught up in furthering religion without a relationship with God, Jesus said:

Woe to you scribes and Pharisees, hypocrites! For you travel across land and sea to win a single convert, and when he becomes one, you make him twice as much a child of hell as yourselves.

(Matthew 23:15)

A relationship founded on righteousness and genuine faith in Christ is what God desires, not a lifeless religious duty. When we come to God in true worship, the shackles of cherished sin cannot come along without being dealt with.

Look at what God had to say to the priests in Malachi's day who had strayed from true instruction in favor of those in power who could benefit them financially and politically:

 Read Malachi 2:5-8 in your Bible.

● What was God looking for from the religious leadership of the day? What was God calling out as harmful in their leadership of the people? What harmful things might God call out in church leadership today?

At the center of the problem in Malachi lay the very heart of worship. Vain offerings have other intentions than to praise God with abandon. We want God to act on our behalf, so we sing some songs and attend church services regularly for a time. That should be enough, right? What is at the heart of that kind of worship? Self. One of the hardest things to do is to abandon the cravings of self-satisfaction in anything, even in the worship of God. God hates that vain, selfish expression in our worship and speaks plainly about it in the prophets because He is not a part of that "worship" at all. No strength, healing, or transformation can happen then. It is our selves that get the worship. All the blustery activity of godless worship accomplishes short-lived gain and wearies all who undertake it.

The next time we are in a worship service let's ask ourselves, "Am I truly worshiping God and letting everything go into His hands?" Let Him meet you there at the heart of true worship and lavish on you His unending love and mercy. That is what He wants to do more than anything! Set your self aside. Yield to His work in your life and just see what God will do in the midst of true worship from a sincere and repentant heart.

- What does true worship from a sincere and repentant heart require from us? Why is it easy to let worship of God drift into a robotic and tiresome action?

FROM THE TWELVE

We as churchgoing Christians might bristle at the idea that we may show contempt for God in how we treat Him, but it is actually very easy to do. English Reformation leader Thomas Cranmer considered a three-step approach when he said, "What the heart desires, the will accepts, and the mind justifies."[1] If our desires are allowed to plume and overshadow us, it is a real challenge for our will to overcome them. If the will is weak because the flesh is strong, the mind is the final battlefield. The mind can be bent to justify the will of the flesh and desire of the heart fairly easily, I hate to say. It's possible you may know exactly what I'm talking about. Dragging around that kind of dead spiritual weight will wear us out and keep us from intimacy with God in prayer. When our desire, will, and mind are captive to something other than Christ, things will not go well. In humble confession and repentance, all three must be put under His lordship and careful work of healing. Just as in Malachi's day, that reconciliation through Jesus will change things in our lives but only for the better. Only for the better.

(page 317-318)

A VERY SMALL WORD WITH A VERY BIG IMPACT

The word "why" is only three letters, but asked at the right time, it can cause deep reflection on our perspective and reasoning. The question that God seemed to ask in Zechariah 7 and 8 is a very small one with a very big impact: **why** were they doing what they were doing in the first place?

ZECHARIAH 520 B.C & AFTER

Zechariah and Haggai were the Minor Prophet dynamic duo. They both spoke during a challenging time in the life of God's people. After the exile was over, God brought His people back to Jerusalem to rebuild the temple and live under His blessing once again. The work God called them to do was continually opposed both politically and socially by the neighboring people in the area. God's people were growing spiritually weary from the weight of the opposition and needed to hear from God in a powerful way. Zechariah pulled back the curtains on the work of God to reveal that God is not only sovereign ruler over the whole world, He is actively working on behalf of His people to sustain, protect, and bless them no matter what the kings of the earth had to say about it. Even so, God's people sometimes required a strong word from Him in order to shift their perspective to higher things.

Some returning exiles that lived not far from Jerusalem came to Zechariah to ask what seemed to be a very simple question. For almost seventy years since the fall of Jerusalem, they had been fasting in the fifth month of every year to remember and mourn the destruction of the temple. It's likely that every Jew in exile did this while in Babylon during that time. The question these men were asking was something like, "We've been fasting the fifth month out of every year over the loss of the temple. Now that we're on the road to building it back, do we need to keep on fasting or do we not have to worry with that anymore?" The general tone of the question seemed to strike a sour note with Zechariah (and God). The response took two chapters to unload, and it blew those guys back in their seats.

> Then the word of the Lord of hosts came to me:
> Say to all the people of the land and the priests, "When you fasted and mourned in the fifth month and in the seventh for these seventy years, was it for me that you fasted? And when you eat and you drink, do you not eat for yourselves and drink for yourselves?"
> (Zechariah 7:4-6)

Here's where that little three-letter word brought some perspective. God acknowledged that they did express themselves in a religious fashion, and not just in the fifth month but in the seventh month, too. They certainly would have looked like fine religious folks on the outside. The fact is, however, that God's knows everything, including the motivation of our hearts. So he dropped that little three-letter word on them to answer their question with His own: **why** were you fasting in the first place? Who were you doing all of that for?

Religious devotion can easily be about something other than God. In fact, wrongly motivated religious devotion gets God as angry as anything because of its dishonesty, deviancy, and ability to do great damage to others. Answering the "why" question in our motivation is key when it comes to spiritual health and a well-cultivated faith.

Things go sideways in work or in life, and our response may be to plead before God for Him to set things back in order just so that we may get back to old familiar patterns. We have a health scare so we pull out all the stops to make sure God notices how religious we are so that He'll make us strong again, only to put Him out of our minds once the all-clear is given. Is that fervent religious expression for God or for us? It may sound more like patronizing flattery if the "why" isn't clear. How might it feel if the only time your spouse is nice to you is when they want something you can give them? Not so great. The question of why we do what we do before God is a deeply personal one. It says a lot about what we think of Him and what we think of ourselves.

- How does the "why" behind our service to God say a lot about what we think of Him? What can it say about what we think of ourselves?

Making God a *part* of a religious life without truly coming near to Him at all is not difficult. Religious tradition that espouses meaning and devotion without truly acknowledging God's ways is everywhere. In Zechariah, the question of true devotion to God seems to come down to one other little word: love. That begs the question: what motivates us in how we relate to God? In answer to the little question "Why?" when considering what we do in expressions of faith, is the answer for us, "Because I truly love God"? That is the only answer that will suffice.

CONCLUSION AND TAKEAWAYS

Walking in genuine faith with God is key to His blessing in our lives and our growth in Christ today. Trying to be clever and justifying our actions that keep hurting us (as well as others) is not the way to walk faithfully in the victory Christ has won over the brokenness of sin. Being genuine requires us to open up to God about every area of our lives and let Him work as only He can to make us into the men and women He means for us to be in Christ. It may not be easy work, but it's always good work that He does in us!

- What are your takeaways from this study? What made the most impact for you?

- What are next steps God is leading you toward in walking through those things with Him? What may need to change for you? What conversations might you need to have with someone?

THIS IS
UNCOMFORTABLE
ACCEPTING THE HARD
WORDS OF GOD

WEEK

3

T he Minor Prophets often get a bad rap. Many think they are only full of wrath and judgment, lacking any love or hope for the future. Nothing could be further from the truth. If you really want to see the love of God on full display, outside of the Gospels, there is likely no better place than the Minor Prophets. Generation after generation God had called to His people to listen to Him and follow His ways of peace. He still does so in Christ to us today. The reason the Minor Prophets are so explicit is that God's people weren't listening. They were racing headlong into ruin. Sometimes God has to turn up His volume in order to get our attention. His strong words in these prophetic books do just that, but they are not words meant to wound. They are words meant to heal. The question is: are we listening?

Let's get comfortable with the uncomfortable in this section and learn to listen for the tender love of our gracious God in the often misunderstood Minor Prophets.

God's words that He gave to these men still speak loudly, powerfully, and will be great encouragers for us as much as anything else in Scripture.

WORDS THAT WOUND: WORDS THAT HEAL

Have you had those people in your life who have said things that you still carry around as scars? Maybe a coach, relative, or other authority figure? Maybe a friend who wasn't thinking? In any case, words can do more lasting damage to the mind and soul than just about anything. James 3 is pretty clear about that. The tongue can do a lot of damage to the soul. Words that wound for the sole purpose of wounding are bad. People may try to dominate, belittle, shame, or dismiss another person with wounding words. We all know what that's like. And, be honest, we have wounded intentionally with our words sometimes, too. But can words wound with the intention of healing?

Here's something to tuck away when you're reading the Bible. God's words to His people are ALWAYS meant to heal and bring us closer to Him. That includes the Minor Prophets. Healing words can be sweet and tender like many in the Psalms and the prayers of Paul. Healing words can also be difficult and even offensive at first. But God never wounds just to wound us. If He ever does wound with His words, it's because we probably won't listen to a nicer way because we're persistent in rebellion and selfishness of some kind. In short, we're hard headed. So take the tough words from God for what they are: healing words.

Look at these words from Hosea about the rebellious Northern Kingdom of Israel (Ephraim is the area where its capital was located):

> I know Ephraim,
>   and Israel is not hidden from me;
> for now, O Ephraim, you have played
>   the whore;
>   Israel is defiled.
> Their deeds do not permit them
>   to return to their God.
> For the spirit of whoredom is within

them,
and they know not the Lord.

(Hosea 5:3-4)

Things had truly sunk to a low level for God to have to speak this
way to His people. In business, politics, religious life, and in the
community everything was "for sale." What guided their every move
was what they could gain from the transaction and what should
have been done for good was prostituted and perverted for personal
gain. People were getting hurt in the process, and God's name was
being dragged through that immoral mud. The reason for God's
strong message here is revealed in verse 11 of the same chapter:
His people were "determined to go after filth." God knows where
that road leads. He turned up the volume here to get His people's
attention. His words here were meant to wound but in order to
encourage repentance and reconciliation. In these healing words
spoken later, look at what God wanted for His people instead:

Sow for yourselves righteousness;
   reap steadfast love;
   break up your fallow ground,
for it is the time to seek the Lord,
   that he may come and rain righ-
      teousness upon you.

(Hosea 10:12)

God's hard words were meant to get His people's attention and call
them to a reconciling work of blessing and steadfast love. What
they were doing was reaping just the opposite. God wanted to rain
righteousness down upon His people and does today as well, but it
requires that we leave ways of wickedness behind and pursue Christ
instead. His strong words here still speak with the same shocking
effect in a time where the battle over worldly cultural influence
upon the church is very real.

- Why do you think people try to avoid the portions of
  Scripture that are more direct and straightforward about sin

and its ill effects? Why might the Minor Prophets be seen as offensive to some?

- Do you remember a time when you heard a hard word from God, your spouse, or from a true friend? What was that like to hear that word?

One thing I have also learned from the Twelve (as well as from experience) is that God is serious about sin. He hates it. He knows what it does to us—to twist and darken and ruin our hearts. He is no friend to prideful boasting. Just because love is at the root of the Minor Prophets doesn't mean to take God's words lightly. He will still speak loudly against destructive and divisive sinful behavior because He loves us too much to not be clear about where sin will take us.

And as we've seen, a just God must act in judgment on the wickedness of sin in our lives. And God surely did pour out His fearsome wrath on your sin and mine. He spared no judgment, turned no bind eye, left no stiff-necked sin unanswered. He poured out His wrath fully on His Son Jesus at Calvary instead of on you and me. Remember that as we go. God's judgment is real. Oh, but thank God, so is His mercy on you and me through Christ Jesus our Redeemer.

CONSIDER YOUR WAYS

One of the most annoying things that can happen, in my view, is when you lay out a list of problems you're facing at the moment and also how you're avoiding dealing with any of them to your own detriment because you just want the problems to go away, and somebody says with his chin dropped and head turned to the side, "Well, how's that working out for you?" It's obviously NOT working out for me. As much as I might want someone to pat me on the shoulder and say nice things instead, maybe what I really need to hear is that annoying comment to snap me out of my funk. Especially when good work is being jeopardized by our inaction and avoidance, a strong word to kick us back into gear may be just the thing.

HAGGAI 520 B.C.

Haggai spoke his strong message (alongside Zechariah) to God's people after God had brought them back to Jerusalem following a time of exile in a far off country because of persistent rejection of

God's ways in favor of sinful and destructive ones. It was time to start again on the right foot this time under God's presence and blessing on all He called them to do. The neighboring peoples, however, did everything they could to hinder, thwart, and discourage God's people from doing God's will in rebuilding the temple. God sent Haggai and Zechariah to breathe new life into the effort. Zechariah detailed the spiritual importance of what God was bringing about. Haggai was there to blow the whistle and get God's people off the couch and back to work!

The major issue in Haggai is that the rebuilding work God specifically called His people to do was being sidelined. Ezra stated that the work was, "by decree of the God of Israel" (Ezra 6:14). The return from exile in Babylon back to Jerusalem had purpose in it, and rebuilding the temple was a big part of that purpose. Today as Christians we don't have a central geographic location that necessarily shapes our spiritual identity as the Jews of that day did with the temple in Jerusalem. We might see the emphasis on temple rebuilding as a little strange. What's the big deal here? Haggai referred to the temple as the house of God. Noted Biblical scholar Thomas McComiskey sheds light on the historical and theological context in saying:

> The house was the outward form of the real presence of the
> Lord among his people. To refuse to build the house was
> at best saying that it did not matter whether the Lord was
> present with them. At worst it was presuming on divine
> grace, that the Lord would live with his people even though
> they willfully refused to fulfill the condition of his indwelling
> that he had laid down.[1]
>
> (McComiskey, *Haggai*)

We can better understand Haggai's sense of outrage. The response of God's people to hardship revealed a less than robust faith in His ability to see it through. But we can act the same way today. God calls us to a mighty work, and when everything doesn't go our way all the time, we opt for something different that is much easier and makes us feel better—like abandoning ministry to busy ourselves redecorating the house into a super comfy hangout. In fact, that was exactly what God's people did in Haggai's day. They said it wasn't the best time right now to do what God had called them to do. They did have time for themselves, however:

> These people say the time has not yet come to rebuild the house of the Lord. Is it a time for you yourselves to dwell in your paneled houses while this house lies in ruins?
> (Haggai 1:2,4)

I think the operative term here is "priorities." God moved heaven and earth to bring "these people" (Haggai 1:2) back from exile into their homeland, and what should have been priority number one got put into the "maybe later" pile. McComiskey is spot on. The attitude seemed to have been, "Things aren't great, but they aren't terrible. God isn't super necessary right now. And God will bless us whether we do what He calls us to or not, especially if what He calls us to is difficult." How do you think that made God feel?

● Is there something you feel strongly that God is urging you to do? Is there a conversation you know you should have with someone, but you've been putting it off because it may be difficult or you're waiting for the "right time"?

God seemed to be saying, "You say now is not the time to attend to the house of the Lord, but your own houses surely have gotten a lot of your attention. Nice paneling, sir." I can confess that I have been guilty of letting my own interests, goals, achievements, and status-seeking get between God and me. I can get my eyes on what the world offers pretty easily. Chasing after that shiny stuff makes us selfish and competitive with our fellow men rather than compassionate and serving. God seemed to address that kind of attitude here. In the next verse, God said something very arresting: "Now, therefore, thus says the Lord of hosts: Consider your ways" (Haggai 1:5). Literally that means, "Take to heart how things are going for you." Set your heart upon it, not in an emotional sense but in an intellectual sense. Think about where your life choices are leading you right now. Abandoning God's work because it is difficult at times doesn't solve any problems. That takes our focus off of what God is doing in our day and for the future for all those who will come after us.

FROM THE TWELVE

Expectations can be good if they drive us to be better. Expectations can be bad if they are unrealistic or used as a tool against someone. I know one marriage counselor who has soon-to-be-married couples do something interesting. He wraps two packages up and writes on the outside of each one "expectations" and then has both fiancées walk over to the window, open it up, and throw the packages right out. Sometimes our conceived expectations can blind us from the beauty of the real thing right in front of us.

God doesn't always work in ways that we expect.
(page 147)

What God was planning to do there in Jerusalem would make the majesty and beauty of Solomon's temple pale in comparison, even if the rebuilt one was less grand in appearance. The old temple was gone. But the house of God still had purpose for Him. That purpose was to give peace (Haggai 2:9). It was there that God would meet His people and accept atonement for their sins. It was there that His ways of peace would be proclaimed to the nations around them. And it was there, in a time to come, where the footsteps of Jesus Christ would fall as He taught, witnessed to, and declared His Gospel of peace for all men. The house of God had far greater priorities than the houses of men could even dream of. Do not ever forget that. In Christ today, if we leave the task unfinished and the work of the Gospel undone, we are working against the blessing of God in our lives and in the world. We work against God if we set His ways to the side in favor of our own selfish ways. Going to church every Sunday isn't the mark of a true follower of Christ. The mark of a true follower is found in the priority of His Gospel in everything we do. We have no idea of the wonderful things God is doing to bring peace to this world through Jesus even today! So Haggai says, "You better think about it!" And don't just think about it. Get up and get to work! There is much to do, and you are part of it. You have a very important part of the work that God is doing to bring peace. How? He will accomplish it by His Spirit *through* you. So no more wasting time on the temporary. We have things to do!

PREPARE

 Read Amos 4:4-13 in your Bible.

The book of Amos reveals the fierce love of God even for His wayward people. In Hosea, God said that He gave His people all of the things they needed, but they thanked their pagan gods for them instead. He gave and gave, but they would not return to Him. Now in Amos, God didn't bring blessings; He brought hardship and want. God was clear: He was bringing the hardship upon them to get His people's attention. However, the harder things became, the more His people turned away from Him. "Yet you did not return to me," God lamented repeatedly throughout Amos chapter 4. Whether times were good or times were bad, God was left out. Their thankless hearts were indicative of growing evil and rebellion within. Thankfulness is the big indicator as to where we are in our walk with the Lord. It may seem small, but it's the fruit of a healthy relationship with God. It shows how much or how little we think of God. Remember Jesus in Luke 17 when He healed ten lepers and only one came back to say thank you? And the one who came back wasn't even among the people of Israel. He was from another region altogether. It's very telling of God's people that this outsider was the only thankful one. Jesus replied, "Were not ten cleansed? Where are the nine? Was no one found to return and give praise to God except this foreigner?" (Luke 17:18-19) The thanklessness of God's people (we included) can be appalling.

- It's easy to get busy with everyday life and take for granted the blessings of God in Christ to us today. When have you expressed thankfulness to God recently for all He has done for you?

One of the most terrifying statements God made in the whole Bible comes up next. In the face of His own people's blatant rebellion, injustice, cruelty, perversity, and greed, God said He would personally bring the might of His wrath on this haughty nation in judgment. He said this in no uncertain terms:

> Therefore this will I do to you, O Israel,
> because I will do this to you,
> prepare to meet your God, O Israel."
> (Amos 4:12)

Those words were meant to drive people to their knees in prayer. **Let me ask you this question that I have asked myself many times. Is this how God needs to speak to you to get your attention?** Will you listen with a thankful heart as He sings songs of love and care over you? Or do you have to come up against the might of a just God because you keep burning it down in your sin and selfishness, dragging His name and yours through the mud? Come on, let's be real together. Are you hardheaded and stubborn in your sin? Always remember God's character: He wants us to return to Him in full confession and repentance so that He can pour out His blessings on us in peace. He is not mean and nasty. He is just. Who would want an unjust God except those who want a free pass to do whatever they feel like doing no matter what? People of conscience want a just God. But He is merciful, too. Only God can balance those two so perfectly.

A.W. Tozer had a great quote. He believed what says the most about a person "is not what he at any given time may say or do, but what he in his deep heart conceives God to be like" (Tozer, *Knowledge of the Holy*).[2] That's a huge predictor of how someone will act in any situation. If they have a low view of God, they'll likely not consider Him with great importance in how they live and think. A high view of God will shape the life and mind towards a Biblical and abundant life in Christ. When Amos dropped the fact that God said to prepare for His judgment, how did the people of the Northern Kingdom respond? What did they conceive God to be like? This is very telling.

> Then Amaziah the priest of Bethel sent to Jereboam king of Israel saying, "Amos has conspired against you in the midst of the house of Israel. The land is not able to bear his words."

And Amaziah said to Amos, "O seer, go, flee away to the land of Judah and eat bread there, and prophesy there, but never again prophesy at Bethel, for it is the king's sanctuary, and it is a temple of the kingdom."

(Amos 7:10, 12-13)

This priest called Amos' words a conspiracy and ran to the king once his message turned against the Northern Kingdom. The king was that priest's higher authority. He then shouted for Amos to turn around and go back where he came from. He declared that Bethel was the king's sanctuary for that kingdom. The words of God were not welcome there, especially if they didn't have glowing things to say. In short, they didn't think much of God. They did think much of Assyria, though. Remember Hosea saying, "Ephraim (the Northern Kingdom) is like a dove, silly and without sense, calling to Egypt, going to Assyria" (Hosea 7:11). Like a silly dove they cooed and wooed the very pagan nation that was about to wipe them out. There's a lesson there. God decried their apathetic and indifferent attitude towards Him. In the face of all their opposition, Amos shouted God's message:

I hate, I despise your feasts,
and I take no delight in your solemn
assemblies.

Take away from me the noise of your
songs,
to the melody of your harps, I will not
listen.
But let justice roll down like waters,
and righteousness like an ever-flowing
stream.

(Amos 5:21, 23-24)

God isn't looking for fake faith and religious junk. He's looking for justice and righteousness that come out of a real faith in Him. He wants people who will listen when He speaks to them. There is no stopping His justice and righteousness any more than a man can stand in the middle of river and prevent its flowing by shouting and holding up his hand.

How do you respond to the words of God in Amos? What do you conceive Him to be like? If there is something smothering your faith and crippling the abundant life you have in Christ, let Him reveal it. Don't dodge the hard words of God. Let them draw you to His side with greater speed and love than even His most tender words. Know His character. He works for your good through Christ our Lord, even in the furnace.

- Do the hard words of God make you want to come to Him or to run from Him? What do you think motivates those feelings? How does knowing God's character help us to see the goodness of God even His hard words?

- What we perceive God to be like is a huge predictor of how we respond and make choices in a given situation. How does having a high or low view of God play into how we might respond to the hard words of God?

CONCLUSION AND TAKEAWAYS

Walking in genuine faith with God is key to His blessing in our lives and our growth in Christ today. Trying to be clever and justifying our actions that keep hurting us (as well as others) is not the way to walk faithfully in the victory Christ has won over the brokenness of sin. Being genuine requires us to open up to God about every area of our lives and let Him work as only He can to make us into the men and women He means for us to be in Christ. It may not be easy work, but it's always good work the He does in us!

- What are your takeaways from this study? What made the most impact for you?

- What are next steps God is leading you toward in walking through those things with Him? What may need to change for you? How might you communicate these ideas with someone who may struggle with the hard words of God?

PERSPECTIVE
GOD'S WAY IS ALWAYS BETTER

From the very beginning with Adam and Eve right on through to our own day, the temptation to take over and be the one to call the shots is ever present. The problem comes when we're focused on everyone else's doing what they're "supposed to do" and forget about the molding and shaping that we ourselves need as Christians. It's not difficult to fall into a pattern of complacency and letting things slide that end up really hurting us (as well as others) as they build up into spiritual stumbling blocks. It's hard to run the race marked out for us in Christ Jesus (Hebrews 12:1) when we're tripping over ourselves half the time.

Happily, the Minor Prophets don't have a problem assisting us in noticing the junk that we let pile up in our own lives. In fact, they are best friends to us in doing so because that sinful junk can ruin everything if we let it stay. Sometimes, the unhealthy patterns we create for ourselves can be very difficult to part with because we've become so used to them. Only our gracious God and loving Savior can walk with us through that process to find true freedom and victory in Jesus' name. Here, the Minor Prophets share words of truth and grace that come from the heart of God Himself to throw off what weighs us down. Then we can follow His paths of strength and right fellowship with Him.

LESSER GODS

ZEPHANIAH 640-610 B.C

Zephaniah spoke toward the end of the Southern Kingdom of Judah. His warnings were stern, and yet his statements about the enduring love of God are beautiful and timeless. His voice was among the last to be heard speaking God's words to His people before their rebellion brought His judgment with the fall of Jerusalem in 586 B.C. God was calling to His people yet again to turn from their ways marked by wickedness, corruption, and immorality and to return to Him who cared for them more than they could ever know. This mighty Minor speaks loudly to us today with the same sobering but hopeful message.

In my view, Zephaniah is dialed right in to a prevailing attitude in our modern world, at least in the West. Zephaniah stated it plainly enough:

> At that time…I will punish the men
> who are complacent,
>   those who say in their hearts,
> "The Lord will not do good,
>   nor will he do ill."
>
> (Zephaniah 1:12)

The imagery used here is interesting. The phrase translated "complacent" is literally "thickening on the dregs" in Hebrew. In making wine, the sediment (or dregs) had to be separated out from the wine itself or else it would thicken the wine making it undrinkable. **Leaving all the junk in there ruined everything in**

the process of developing a good wine. The junk had to go or else everything would be ruined—in winemaking as well as in life.

Those who "thickened on the dregs" in life just sat back and left the work half done. The corrosive impurities stayed. Why would they do that? Zephaniah hit the nail on the head: they said in their hearts that God was not going to do anything either way no matter what they chose. God was a nice idea but not a force to be reckoned with. "I can control my own destiny and don't need a God when I have myself and my self-sufficiency to worship. Lesser gods are fine with me, and I've made peace with whatever might offend God. I want to be left alone in my perceived security, thank you very much," is what this attitude may have sounded like.

One commentary says this about this idea of thickening on the dregs:

> The metaphor in the book of Zephaniah refers to those who have lived with uninterrupted prosperity and have become complacent. These are people who have deified themselves, thinking their might and the power of their hands have gotten them wealth (Deut 8:10-18). Many of Jerusalem's citizens had remained in their apostate lifestyle so long that they had become satisfied with it and then grown indifferent to genuine piety.[1]
>
> (Barker and Bailey, *Zephaniah*)

What was going on in Zephaniah's day to warrant this kind of speech against God's people? The short introduction to Zephaniah (called a superscription) is unusual among the Minors in that it revealed a short lineage of his family history. He was related to a "Hezekiah," and many believe that referred to the king of Judah in Micah's day. If that's true, Zephaniah and the king of his own day, Josiah, were cousins. What Zephaniah was talking about then wasn't some vague idea. These things happened right in front of him and his family. The leadership had sunk to godless corruption and apostasy. God had been kicked out of Jerusalem, or so it seemed.

2 Chronicles 33 related the moral and spiritual downfall of God's people in Jerusalem just before Zephaniah spoke. The Southern Kingdom had a horrible king named Manasseh along with his horrid son Amon. Kings, judges, scribes, and priests fell to all-time lows in perversity and wickedness under their leadership. They did what was right in their own eyes. Verse 10 summed it up: "The Lord spoke to Manasseh and to his people, but they paid no attention." Exactly. The leadership had a deal with the pagan nation of Assyria that cost them a lot, but they made it work by passing the price of tribute off on the people of God with taxes. The temple was decorated with the pagan images of Assyria and was eventually closed. Children were thrown into the fire in an attempt to appease these grotesque man-made gods. What God desired and brought about for their good was cast aside in lust for power, money, pleasure, and security. "You can talk all you want, God, but this works for me. This feels right to me. This makes me money. I have international credibility. It might be messy for the poor people, but whatever. The system works for me." They were fine with God as long as He kept His mouth shut on what they were doing.

- Have you experienced this kind of complacent attitude? Where? How was that attitude expressed in words or actions?

Woe to her who is rebellious and defiled,
   the oppressing city!
She listens to no voice;
   she accepts no correction.
She does not trust the Lord;
   she does not draw near to her God.
                        (Zephaniah 3:1-2)

The recipe is as follows: "Stop living for God and go your own way. Don't follow Him. Strike out on your own path without Him, and decide for yourself what is good or evil. Don't inquire of God to act in your life—just do what feels right to you. Trust your feelings. Throw off the perceived restrictions of Godly living and blow the doors off in pursuing your lusts and pleasures. Oppress and deceive others in getting what you want. Don't listen to anyone, especially God or anyone representing Him. Think that everything you do is right or at least can't be criticized because you did what felt good and seemed best at the time. Follow your heart. Do not trust God to lead you. Do not leave your sin behind to draw near to God. Keep Him at a distance."

It's that easy. And people do that every day. The trouble with that recipe for life is that it does not work out well at all from God's perspective.

- God called out "listening to no voice" and "accepting no correction." Why is that so dangerous? How do those actions lead to not trusting God and not drawing near to Him?

The things we create and idolize to provide some sense of security and self worth become the very devils that hound us, tear at us, and ruin the things that make life worth living. Lesser gods always disappoint and steal from us what we thought they would provide.

Being honest, we can tend to think very highly of ourselves and praise our own sense of justice and what should be morally acceptable in society and in religious life. We can do the "church thing" just fine without God or the Bible getting in the way. We can order our world and impose systems upon it that reflect our personal sense of what is good and just and fair—divorced from God. Any student of history can tell you how often mankind has tried that. Pride and arrogance fuel the selfish heart and always lead it to destruction, both on a personal level and on a national level. We desperately, entirely, and unquestionably need God to lead us every single day. It does not turn out well when we try to lead ourselves.

REND YOUR HEARTS AND NOT YOUR GARMENTS

Spending meaningful time with the brutally honest Minor Prophets definitely has an effect. Don't mistake me: it's a good one! But it isn't easy. Being open and real are things we hear a lot about in contemporary society, but those are rare qualities to find. Even rarer to find those who have truly cultivated them. To many today, being open and real means you say whatever comes to mind regardless of present company (preferably with some attitude). Today you need an aloof attitude towards sin and its effects, applauding any mode of self-expression because to not applaud would be judgmental. We like to be identified as open and real through the image we build online and in our societal groups, but what we build is a façade and not a structure with any foundation. Try expressing an opinion that runs counter to pop morality, and you'll get hammered for speaking openly about it. Being open and real fall under the title of "cool" today. But "cool" is essentially a fake front for the soul-killing vanity encouraged by our rootless culture. Being open and real are the deadliest weapons to the sinful self. They are not "cool." Those two expose everything.

JOEL 800s - 700s B.C

Joel's message is one that is difficult for scholars to put a date on. He spoke about a great locust plague that had apparently just happened and devastated the land. He also spoke of a great human army that was on the way to wreak further havoc on God's people. Joel came to declare that those events were nothing less than God's judgment on His people over their sinful actions and repeated rejection of His ways of peace in the Law. The message was clear: stop doing those things and return to God and be spared His further judgment. Joel didn't list the offenses God's people were committing, but he did provide the way out—sincere and heartfelt repentance.

The below verses in Joel are the great doorway to the rest of his book. Here was where he got truly open and real. He didn't give us a list of offensive things that were being done at the time that incurred God's wrath. He only gave the remedy. That meant that God was not only after a simple change in actions or outward appearance; the remedy went right to the heart. Literally.

> "Yet even now," declares the Lord,
>   "return to me with all your heart,
> with fasting, with weeping, and with
>   mourning,

117

> and rend your hearts and not your
>   garments."
> Return to the Lord your God,
>   for he is gracious and merciful,
> slow to anger, and abounding in
>   steadfast love,
> and he relents over disaster.
>
> (Joel 2:12-13)

Earlier in the book of Joel the prophet described a swarm of locusts sent by God that had come and devastated the land. And now approaching was a mighty human army sent because God could no longer let His people's wickedness go on as it had. What did God say next? Did He sit back to watch the carnage? No. He said this: "'Yet even now,' declares the Lord, 'return to me.'" What could have been going on in the culture that had carried God's people away from Him in their words, thoughts, and deeds? Joel doesn't really say. We may tend to get focused on what we are doing that's wrong—asking God all kinds of questions and psychoanalyzing everything. Questioning and trying to understand aren't wrong, but when they become our sole focus, to fix it ourselves or to figure it out, God gets left out. He's not the focus then; we are. God knows that, more than anything, we need the fountain of living water, His comforting and transforming Holy Spirit, filling the deepest parts of our hearts and souls. What we need is *Him*. "Return to *me*," He says.

It reminds me of what Jesus said in the Gospels:

> Come to me all you who labor and are heavy laden, and I will give you rest. Take my yoke upon you and learn from me, for I am gentle and humble in heart, and you will find rest for your souls. For my yoke is easy, and my burden is light.
>
> (Matthew 11:28-30)

Not "Come to a warped religious framework that you use to cloak your brokenness"; not "Come to a logical pattern of thought that

118

makes sin less offensive and more palatable"; not "Come to a system that tells you everything is all right when it isn't." He said, "Come to me and I will give you rest." Our mighty Minor reflected that call to come before God. Today we go to the person of Jesus in confession and repentance. Joel wasn't interested in games, fake faith, or pretty sounding words that didn't mean anything. Faith must be open and real.

 Read Joel 2:12-17 in your Bible.

The phrase Joel used here at the end was only used once in the whole Bible, and it is powerful:

> return to me with all your heart,
> with fasting, with weeping, and with
> mourning,
> and rend your hearts and not your
> garments.
>
> (Joel 2:12-13)

Returning to God through the grace of Jesus after we've wandered away into the darkness has to be done with our whole heart. Have you had those times when you've come face-to-face with something you've done that you know broke God's heart? Perhaps you developed sinful patterns that consistently drew you away from God. Returning to God like the prodigal son did, falling on our knees and confessing the ruin we have created for ourselves is painful. It is also the doorway to freedom in Christ today. Joel said in 1:8 to lament like a virgin whose fiancé died tragically just before the day of their wedding. It is the recognition of great loss. Sin steals so much from us. Joel called the whole Jewish nation of his day to fasting, weeping, and mourning. That may not sound like much fun, but being open and real with God turns the hardened soil of a fallow heart and plants seeds of rich spiritual fruit that will last, nourishing everyone.

● Are there some sinful areas in your life that you haven't given to God? Are you still hanging on to those thoughts, practices, and patterns? Don't feel judged—we all struggle with this at some point in our journey of being made more like Christ through faith. What keeps you from "being open and real" with God?

In the whole of Scripture, only here in Joel does this phrase occur — "rend your hearts and not your garments." In Joel's day, tearing one's clothes was a sign of abject grief. Clothes were often symbolic of status or wealth. People back then did not have a closet full of clothes as we often do today. They may have had only one garment. To tear it had many layers of meaning. Even to us today Joel dives deeply. Tear your heart over your sin. Not just an outward sign of grief. God looks on the heart. He knows if we're being real or not. How seriously do we take our rebellious actions? How seriously do we take the cross of Christ? Taking off our masks before Christ and laying aside our pride with a heartfelt recognition of the destructiveness of our sin is the pathway to freedom. Don't be afraid to take it.

A SONG FOR THE AGES

Every songwriter dreams of writing that one hit song that has a timeless message and quality that delights listeners generation after generation. The final portion of Habakkuk is a timeless and beautiful song of faith in God. In fact, I own a page from a brightly colored prayer book made in 14th century France that some pious (and well to do) person carried with them to worship services or in times of personal prayer. You know what prayer is written on the illuminated page that I have framed? Habakkuk 3:17-19. A song for the ages indeed. We'll look at it in a minute. This song has encouraged countless people of faith over centuries through every up and down of life. Especially through times of great hardship and pain, God's way through is the only way to life and redemption. Trying to chart our own pathway out just makes us more lost and weary. Leaning on God's righteousness and trusting His paths forward through Christ is the only way to overcome.

HABAKKUK c. 615 B.C.

Habakkuk had a powerful conversation with God just a few decades before the fall of Jerusalem (586 B.C). Though just three short chapters, his book has brought comfort to countless numbers of people over history who are having to endure difficult days. He pulls no punches and understands that hard times come, but in the book God gives Habakkuk and us an amazing promise that God will sustain those who seek Him no matter what is going on around us. God will not forget us and will see us through if we will only trust Him through Christ Jesus our hope.

A lot of people in Jerusalem in Habakkuk's day didn't care to hear anything God had to say. Many would never believe that God would allow His own city to be overrun by filthy Babylonians as Habakkuk predicted. They might remark at Habakkuk's words but wouldn't change any current course of living. They preferred their own alternatives to God's design, forfeitures that eased the blow of the repercussions of sinful rebellion. Habakkuk knew how hard the days to come would be for so many when called to account, but God gave him a strong word to share with those who followed Him each day: *I will sustain you Myself.* The power of the song that followed in response has found its voice among untold numbers of people of faith through the years living in dark times and fearful days. Look how Habakkuk opened the song.

> O Lord, I have heard the report of you,
>   and your work, O Lord, do I fear.
> In the midst of the years revive it;
>   in the midst of the years make it
>   known.
> In wrath remember mercy.
>
> (Habakkuk 3:2)

Habakkuk knew with whom he was dealing. He did not take the word of God nor His actions lightly. He trusted God's promises in every season, good and bad. He had read and heard about the work of God on behalf of His people in the past—especially freeing them from Egypt and defeating Pharaoh's armies, leaving them drowned at the bottom of the sea. Rightly so, Habakkuk is stricken to the heart knowing that God is about to act in might against the prevalent corruption and wickedness of his day. **But He knew God's character. Knowledge of God's character is at the heart of these awesome Minor Prophets.** Habakkuk now knew that something big was brewing. God was doing something for His faithful people again. "In the middle of it all, make us live," is one way to understand the second part of verse two above. Though difficult to translate, the next part of that verse is similar to it: "In the middle of everything, help us understand what You are doing."

122

Habakkuk was a bit fearful of what was to come, but He was not fearful of God's hand in his life. He asked only that God sustain His faithful people, help them understand His ways, and one more thing: remember mercy.

In many translations, the end of verse two reads, "In wrath remember mercy." But the word translated "wrath" reads more like, "in times of trembling, agitation, excitement and disturbance." We can all relate to those kinds of times. Mercy is a must. Sometimes things happen that are very hard to understand or explain. Those can be the most painful days of all. God's mercy is sometimes all we have to hold on to in those times. God revealed clearly what He was doing in Habakkuk's day. The salvation of God's people was secured, but the power of God on display would be an overwhelming thing to behold. "If You know You need to shake things up, Lord, shake them up, but please have mercy on those who trust in You," he says. Happily, God gladly grants mercy today to those who call on His name through Jesus Christ our Savior.

The song of memory of God's mighty works and the pronouncement of what was to come brought a shiver to Habakkuk. The day ahead looked dark indeed. But because of God's faithful promise that the righteous shall *live* by faith (Habakkuk 2:4), Habakkuk looked boldly into the face of a hard future and sang this amazing and timeless song:

> Though the fig tree should not blos-
> som,
> no fruit be on the vines,
>   the produce of the olive fail
>   and the fields yield no food,
> the flock be cut off from the fold
>   and there be no herd in the stalls,
> yet I will rejoice in the Lord;
>   I will take joy in the God of my salva-

tion.

(Habakkuk 3:17-18)

Personally, it wasn't until I began to take God at His word and see Him act in faithfulness through my own hardships that I started to open up to this song for the ages. I guess I'm hardheaded. But I can say now with full confidence that this kind of hope in God is never put to shame. To trust in God in the face of an overwhelming flood of trouble and trial is not the habitation of fools. It is the abode of the survivor, the strong, the son of peace, and the unvanquished. "Yet will I rejoice in the Lord" is foolishness to some. But it requires knowing Him as "the God of my salvation" to understand it. If I am trying to be my own salvation, this song will make no sense and might even make me angry. But to trust God, to breathe deeply and then let my future go from my hands into His is where the strongest souls sing songs like this one. And they are never put to shame. Father, help us to let our future be in your hands and to take joy in You, in good times and in bad. In You alone do we trust through Christ our Savior. Make us live, and help us to understand. Remember mercy, blessed Father. We wait on You.

- Trusting God's ways instead of our own through times of "trembling" and uncertainty can be a challenge. What is the hardest part of trusting God in difficult times for you?

- How have you seen God's faithfulness in your own life during a fearful time or in the life of someone you know? What might the song say that you might sing of God's sustaining you during a personal trial?

CONCLUSION AND TAKEAWAYS

There is true freedom for us in Christ in repentance from the "junk" we have allowed to stay in our patterns of living. Surrendering our will by turning from that junk in repentance and trusting in God's good will for us in Christ is the way to freedom and abundant life in Christ our Lord. Especially in those areas where we are most tempted to look elsewhere for fulfillment, blessing, and life, letting go of the sinful patterns and "junk" may be difficult, but Jesus brings healing and new life where darkness once ruled if we trust Him! God's way is always better.

- What are your takeaways from this study? What made the most impact for you?

● What are next steps God is leading you toward in walking through those things with Him? What may need to change for you? What conversations might you need to have with someone about these things?

5 IDOL FACTORIES
THE TEMPTATION TO REDEFINE GOD

I dol worship may not be something we think about as a regular
practice in our modern world. What we consider idol worship
may happen in less developed countries and backward cultures,
we might think. But from a Biblical point of view, idol worship is
something that not only happens in modern culture, it is a regular
practice. Whenever we create things or turn to people to give us
meaning, identity, purpose, prosperity, "the good life," or an attempt
to acquire what we feel we lack as men and women, we become idol
worshipers. Church reformer John Calvin (1509-1564 A.D.) made
a bold admission of us as humans: he called us "idol factories."[1]
And I hate to admit it, but he was right. It requires very little effort
to become jealous, envious, lustful, greedy and led away by our
sinful desires to become idol makers in our attempt to "complete"
ourselves in our own way.

The theme of idolatry is repeated throughout the Minor Prophets
because, just as in our own day, God's people were idol factories
then as well. The messages of these books ring as true today as they
ever did. And the outcome is the same—idols never bring what we
desire of them. Setting our affections on the shiny distractions of
worldly culture makes for an eye-catching but superficial façade
that often hides a hurting and needy interior.

INSIDE, OUTSIDE, UPSIDE-DOWN

That was the name of a Berenstain Bears book I loved as a kid.[2]
It could also be a good title for what was going on in Samaria
and Jerusalem in the Minor Prophet Micah's day (700s B.C.).
The outside looked nice enough, but man-oh-man that inside
was a real mess and turned upside down completely. God does
not have a problem getting in our personal business if He needs
to, especially if what we're doing hurts others. The Northern and
Southern Kingdoms were proud of their respective cities. They
wanted to show off. The ivory couches and paneled homes of the
wealthy would rival anything in the neighboring nations. Samaria
and Jerusalem were something to be proud of with their gleaming
walls and glittering homes. They had finally "made it." The clothes
of the wealthy were threaded with gold and fine needlework. The
parties were wild and raucous with the town's most prestigious
people filling the night air with drunken laughter and music made
for the times. It may sound fun to some, but it was powered by
something terrible—cruel and brutal oppression. What a shining
socialite might have raised a toast to, God was calling nothing less
than prostitution of all that was good in the world. What they
were proud of, God was deeply ashamed of and offended by. God
got right to the heart of the matter and called the attention of the
whole world to the front door of His own people.

I'm not saying that God is against happiness or prosperity. Not
at all. But let's drill down into what Micah is saying, and I think
we'll see something that we can agree is not good. We may also see
something that is all too familiar in our own day.

It's a bit like a courtroom drama where God was making His case.
This section of Micah is written in a legal complaint style. God was
the witness who would testify to what He had seen.

> All this is for the transgression of
> Jacob
> and for the sins of the house of Israel.

What is the transgression of Jacob?
Is it not Samaria?
And what is the high place of Judah?
Is it not Jerusalem?

(Micah 1:5)

The shining examples these people had poured their wealth, effort, and self-indulgence into had risen to become a hotspot for any travel guide but also a stench in the nostrils of God. The whole thing was inside, outside, upside-down. God called Jerusalem, the place where He said He would put His name forever, a "high place." High places of that time were pagan altars set up on a hilltop in the region for worshiping demonic deities in vile ways. **The disconnect between God and His people was real.** They were fine with it. God was sickened by it. What looked great on the outside was rotten on the inside. Micah was called to not just look at the dazzling front door but to go inside the house to see how things really were. *There was* where the problem lay. It's the same way with us. The outside may look great. How's the inside? What is the real story? God works to redeem and restore us from the inside out. He's not fooled and doesn't want us to fake our faith. Jesus would agree. Look at this:

Woe to you scribes and Pharisees, hypocrites! For you clean the outside of the cup and plate, but inside they are full of greed and self-indulgence. You blind Pharisee! First clean the inside of the cup and the plate, that the outside may also be clean.

(Matthew 23:25-26)

The cup and dish were items used in religious worship of God in the daily services of the temple. Jesus kicked open the front door, as it were, to see what was going on inside. The outside looked clean, but what was inside was "full of greed and self-indulgence." Clean the inside first, Jesus said of their hearts and religious expression, and then the outside would be just as clean. That's a tough one. Billions are spent annually in this country on ways to make the

129

outside look good, Christians included. But if we open the front door of our lives, what will we see? What about the front door of the church we attend?

It's an inside-out job that God does through Christ our Lord to transform and redeem us. That is a consistent theme in all of Scripture. That is also not something we like to consider. We like to keep that front door nicely decorated but definitely closed.

- Why do you think it may be easier to focus on externals than to let God in to work on the inside of our hearts? What draws us to compare ourselves with others?

 Read Micah 3:1-12 in your Bible.

- The first part of this chapter is pretty yucky. Those who suffered under such corrupt political and religious leadership felt no better than stew in the pot of those people. What kind of things did God call out concerning the failed leadership of Micah's day? How might the effects of living under that kind of leadership feel?

Here's the deal: God knows everything. We can never hide anything from Him. That may be uncomfortable at first blush, but how freeing it is to have Him who loves us so much also know what goes on behind the front door of our lives. What's more, He wants to come inside! He wants to work in those neglected and shameful rooms stacked to the ceiling with wounds and hurts from long ago. Micah widely opens the front door. No more hiding all the junk. The way to respond is not to try to slam the door in God's face. He knows everything. Open the door. Just see what wonderful things He will do through a living faith in Christ who makes all things new!

- How might striving to meet the expectations of culture or other people encourage idolatry in our lives?

PRETTY CREATURES DO UGLY THINGS TO PEOPLE

Doctor Zhivago is a movie from the 1960s based on a Boris Pasternak novel about an adulterous relationship between a man and a woman caught up in the whirlwind of the Russian revolution of the early 20th century.[3] It is a sweeping epic. At the beginning of the film, a gruff old doctor is talking to the eager-eyed young Doctor Zhivago and encourages him to get into medical research. The doctor/poet Zhivago responds that he prefers general practice and real life. All of this takes place over a microscope where the young doctor is admiring a strikingly colorful bacteria moving about under the lens, shifting and sliding in determined action of finding a host. Zhivago comments that what he is seeing looks beautiful to him. The gruff old doctor snatches the plate out from under the microscope, holds it up to the light to see the same bacteria Zhivago did and says plainly, "I've found that pretty creatures do ugly things to people." The stage is set for the tragic drama to unfold.

At the end of God's last response to Habakkuk recorded in chapter two, God seemed to go off on a tangent. He had been decrying the pride and haughtiness of the Babylonians and offering woes and taunts that the nations under their domination would sing out once that nation fell. Then suddenly He shifted gears to talk about something that seems off topic—idolatry. It's not off topic at all. In fact idolatry is at the very center of the whole problem. Even today idols are everywhere. They don't have to look like a Babylonian god. They could look like a beautiful human body, wealth, status, or prosperity.

Anything that we put in God's place to bring us pleasure, fulfillment, blessing, or things desired apart from Him becomes an idol. They will bring you down into shame and ruin if you trust them.

Habakkuk shows us why.

Habakkuk mentioned the typical idols of his day: "a metal image," "a wooden thing," and "overlaid with gold and silver" (Habakkuk (2:18,19). **But what is most powerful about an idol is not its form or appearance but its influence, what it means to us, and what we look for in it.** The awful thing is that we project upon these idols ability and power that they do not and cannot posses. Habakkuk records:

What profit is an idol
   when its maker has shaped it,
   a metal image, a teacher of lies?
For its maker trusts in his own cre-
   ation
   when he makes speechless idols!
                        (Habakkuk 2:18)

Today, we can certainly be led away to idols shaped by human hands and a sinful will. Worshiping idols can seem to feel right or even be enjoyable. It's the devastating aftermath that kills us with shame, grief, and disappointment along with the warped mental framework born out of bowing before idols. They poison our relationships. We kneel before an idol of pornography to feel like the sexually alluring people we lust after, and it ruins our minds and hearts so that relationships crumble under the unfulfilled lusts that run unchecked without hope of satisfaction. We can become slaves to an idol of sexual exploration to feel validation by conquest or to feel lovable or to try and heal deep emotional scars only to find the wounds grow deeper and the feelings grow too heavy to bear. We can make an idol out of money, status, power, and intellect to build up our own walls and set ourselves above those by whom we yearn to be worshiped and praised for our accomplishments only to find our relationships thin and untrustworthy with loneliness never far away. We can make idols out of our children, defending our obsessive indulgence to their whims while at the core is a deep need to be loved for being a provider of every need, healer of every hurt, and giver of every good thing only to find our children grow to despise us for our never-ending meddling and vicarious living through their experiences instead of our own which only brings exclusion and not their acceptance. We can make idols out of ourselves, either worshiping our external appearance or cursing it because of perceived inadequacies. In this short list you can see that idols are everywhere. We are sinners and need to be set free from the chains of our idols. But first we have to see them for what they are. Idols, even beautiful ones, will never give you what you think you need from them. They deceive and keep you from God's bountiful blessing and peace—bringing instead your own hurt and destruction.

- Why do you think it is so tempting to look to something else or to someone else to bring us happiness, relief, or blessing instead of to God?

Habakkuk revealed some very timeless truths about idols in any age. He also said some strong things about those who make idols for themselves to replace the Only God. "What profit is an idol when its maker has shaped it, a metal image, a teacher of lies? Can this teach? There is no breath at all in it" (Habakkuk 2:18,19). The idols we make for ourselves do not profit. They will never deliver on the needs we heap upon them. They starve the body, mind, and soul leaving us worse in the end. These images we set up to worship can never give us anything because they are of our own making. They do not rise above their makers or have any power beyond their makers. They do not teach anything to us except the lies that we choose to believe, namely that these idols, be they images, people, or things, will make us better for having worshiped them instead of the Living God. No amount of sincerity or deep belief will make that idol anything more than it is—a dead, dumb, speechless, profitless thing that teaches lies born out of our own sinful pursuit and desire. There is no breath in it. It will never give life for there is none in it. As idols are dead, no matter their form, so they only bring death to the heart and soul of the idol worshiper. Idols will bring you down in tears, not build you up. Lies never bring truth. Do not believe them.

Here's the deal though: you and I both have been idol makers in our lives before. We made idols out of things that we looked to for blessing, prestige, relief, answers, and wealth apart from godliness. Idols are ugly things, and God speaks harshly against them through the whole Bible. Nothing replaces the goodness of an all wise, compassionate, teaching, and healing God. Nothing. That doesn't stop us from turning to things in our sin we would be ashamed for anyone to know about in search of the things only God can give. So what do we do, we idol makers?

First of all, repent of them. Smash those idols. If we have made people into idols, we should ask their forgiveness in tearful confession if possible. If we have made objects into idols, we must get a right perspective on the things God has given us for our good and relate to them without the lust that powers the idol maker. "So how do I do that? That seems like more than I can handle. I'm so used to living with my idols," you might say. And you'd be right. Only the mighty work of God through victorious faith in Jesus Christ can renew our minds and transform our hearts from idol factories into temples of praise to the One God who gives all good things to His beloved sons and daughters (James 1:17). Surrender your heart and mind to Him through Christ in confession and humility. He will make all things new. The difference between an idol and God Almighty is clear: idols lie and profit nothing because they are of our own making, weak and sinful as we are. Those who are on the side of truth and seek for it listen to Jesus, not idols (John 18:37).

God is not made by us. God's ways are "higher that our ways, and His thoughts are higher than our thoughts" (Isaiah 55:8-9). All that we need is found in Him through Christ our Redeemer. In His grace He reaches out to you and to me to abandon our idols and come near to Him through Christ to be filled as only He can fill us. The idols we create out of people and things may be very pretty and lovely in appearance, but pretty creatures do ugly things to people. Idols lie. God does not. Grind your idols into dust in repentance and confession before God. Let Him fill all things in every way. He will through Christ our hope.

- What are some idols you have been tempted to turn to in the past? How did God help you (maybe through a friend or an experience) turn away from that idol and to come to Him through faith in Christ?

WISHING GOD WERE DIFFERENT THAN HE IS

Sometimes it's not idols we create in attempts to shape the world around us to our liking; sometimes we may even try to twist God's words or to make God into someone He is not so we can feel more comfortable about the lives we desire to live. It's as though we try to make God into a "better God" according to our own personal judgments on the world and on other people. When we don't see people and the world around us in the same way that our redeeming and reconciling God does, emotions often get the better of us and in our impatience, we may get frustrated with God and His ways that don't always agree with our feelings on how things should be. As Jonah had to find out, God doesn't disregard our feelings, especially when difficult things have been suffered, but our Good Shepherd leads His dear children along on paths of righteousness that seek to bring healing to our hurts but also hope and restoration to even the least deserving among us.

JONAH c.700s B.C

Jonah lived during a difficult time in Israel's history when the kingdom of Assyria was ravaging that part of the world with oppressive cruelty. God gave Jonah a message to deliver to those very people right in the heart of their capital city of Nineveh. Jonah, however, had other ideas and ran as far away from the call of God as he could. Even the possibility that the people who had inflicted such hardships on his people might be given the opportunity by God to repent was too much for him. Either they faced God's judgment and "got what was coming to them" or Jonah wanted no part of it. The story told in his amazing book is one of God's sovereignty over kings of the earth but also one of God's tenderness to a prophet who had a difficult time understanding that God's goodness extended to all who would hear His voice and repent.

Jonah faithfully delivered the oracle in Nineveh of coming judgment if the evil didn't stop. But it took quite a journey to get there for one big reason: Jonah fled as far away as he could in the opposite direction when God gave him the task. Finally in chapter four Jonah revealed why he ran from God's call to him in the first place.

Assyria had been a kingdom northeast of Israel for a good while before Jonah's day. Earlier kings of that nation had decided to expand their territory by invading neighboring lands and brutally killing those who opposed them. They made examples of peoples that did not submit, inflicting horrific acts of torture and atrocity. They earned a reputation, and city after city paid tribute instead of facing Assyrian brutality. Before Jonah's day, even the Northern Kingdom of Israel paid tribute to them. There is even an ancient obelisk in existence dating from an earlier period showing Jehu, king of Israel, bowing before the Assyrian king at the time in tribute and submission. Jehu took from the temple treasury of God's house to regularly pay off that cruel king. Assyria and its reputation were well known to Jonah. The bowing of a king before such a wicked culture and robbing the people of Israel to pay tribute would be like a stick in anyone's eye that cared for God, Jonah's included. He would have liked to see judgment come to these horrid people who had oppressed Israel and so many others. He had probably been living under Assyrian fear and oppression along with his family and neighbors for many years. Assyria wasn't a far off idea. It was kind of personal.

What Jonah failed to see is that by the Assyrians' ceasing their evil ways of cruelty and oppression he and the people of Israel would be directly affected in measurably positive ways. The Ninevites' listening to God in this matter and acting in accordance with His peaceful design would also benefit everyone around them. But it didn't appear that Jonah could think that way at the moment. He saw only what had come before by their oppression and how hurtful it was. He wanted retribution. He wanted judgment for them for what they had done for so long. The message God gave him to deliver was, "Yet forty days and Nineveh shall be overthrown!" That was what Jonah was hoping for. That hits close to home. In today's deeply judgmental culture, we will dig through a person's past until we come up with something offensive and then demand they pay dearly for it whether or not we were affected by that past decision. We look to repayment of wrongs and the destruction of our offenders. What happens for you the day after all that judgment comes about for them? "I don't care!" we might scream. We want what Jonah wanted. We want the tables turned right now without any regard to the future. Peace tomorrow is not on the agenda. Retribution now is.

● Why is it so difficult to pray for and share God's love with those we deeply disagree with or may even have been wounded by somehow?

Before I sound as if I'm missing the emotional point, I must admit that living through what Jonah's people may have endured for years is not something I have had to experience. The constant reminder of fear and oppression works on a man's soul, no doubt. There are times when we just want things to change and don't care as much about what comes later. "We'll deal with that when we get to it," we say. It's very hard to be future minded when the present is so difficult. 2 Kings records very clearly what it was like to be alive around Jonah's day. It was pretty rough. Leadership in Israel was at a low point, and God had to work through some real meatheads to bless His people at the time. When Jonah was alive, most likely Jeroboam II was king in Israel. Scripture states:

> [Jeroboam] restored the border of Israel from Lebo-Hamath as far as the Sea of the Arabah, according to the word of the Lord, the God of Israel, which He spoke by His servant Jonah the son of Amittai, the prophet, who was from Gath-hepher. For the Lord saw that the affliction of Israel was very bitter, for there was none left, bond or free, and there

was none to help Israel… so He saved them by the hand of Jeroboam the son of Joash.

(2 Kings 14:25-27)

There it is. The people of Israel were "afflicted" and that affliction was "very bitter." There was "none to help Israel." There just weren't friends for Israel around at that time. No one wanted them there. Not a fun time to be alive, especially for a prophet of God trying to encourage his neighbors. If I try to place myself in that mindset, the picture changes a bit. Jonah had no desire whatsoever for the relenting of God's mighty justice on those wicked pagan people in Nineveh. He was actually afraid of that peaceful outcome. He lived in a time of very bitter affliction for his people. He wanted judgment for those who were making life hard for them. In fact, he made a stunning admission to that fact. He revealed his wounded heart when he found out on the forty-first day that God would honor Nineveh's grieving of their evil and changing of their ways— God would relent. They would be spared His judgment. What Jonah said to God in response to that mercy is shocking. He called what God did, "evil" (Jonah 4:1).

- Have you personally experienced feeling that what God wanted in bringing about His will in a situation seemed wrong to you? Have you seen that in others as they seek out their desired view of life? How did God work in that situation?

Biblical scholars are divided on what might have made Jonah angry. Some say he was a nationalistic Jew who wanted the defeat of non-Jewish peoples. Some say Jonah was frustrated by the whole process of delivering a word of warning to a people who didn't care about God in the first place. To me, Jonah sounds somehow personally wounded. The hurt went deep enough to compel him to try to run away from the very presence of God rather than possibly witness God's mercy on Nineveh. It seems that the outcome here personally bothered him. There was a strong disconnect here between the prophet and the God who sent him. Jonah 4:1 literally reads, "It was evil to Jonah with great evil."

We sometimes may want God to be different than He is because of personal feelings that we have about a situation or experience. We may even have very strong opinions on the matter. We might feel like there are some who don't deserve mercy, as though we ourselves do. Why is God "patient with us, not wanting any to perish but all to come to repentance" (2 Peter 3:9)? Sometimes God is not easy to understand right off the bat. However, God sees what we cannot. He knows what we do not. He is above the tossing waves of a broken world, as Jesus demonstrated, though He is very present in it to redeem and restore. He sees beyond the hurtful present into a hopeful future found in Him. We have to trust Him. We know that "He works all things for the good of those who love Him and are called according to His purpose" (Romans 8:28). That doesn't mean that we see the whole picture like He does. Jonah needed an eternal perspective. I relate. It's hard not to be blinded by our own feelings, emotions, and experiences instead of letting God in Christ illuminate the true path that leads to peace with Him.

CONCLUSION AND TAKEAWAYS

As we've seen in spending time with the ol' Minor Prophets, being open and real is a must. The Twelve encourage us to not turn a blind eye to the things that keep tripping us up in our spiritual walk and certainly call attention to ungodly thinking that bears deceptive and malicious fruit in our lives. These Twelve might not be the guys you'd take to a party, but they just might save your life! Let's allow their words to guide our hearts toward Christ our Savior and Redeemer today.

- What are your takeaways from this study? What made the most impact for you?

- What are next steps that God is leading you toward in walking through those things with Him? What may need to change for you? How does this study spark ideas of conversations you might have with someone concerning God?

WEEK

WRECKED AND RESTORED
LIFTING OUR EYES ABOVE THE RUBBLE

I know for me, spending time with the Minor Prophets can shine a spotlight on areas in my life and spiritual walk with Christ that I don't often like to address. Those things I like to overlook are the very ones the Minors call to my attention. If we're not careful, we can miss the full message of restoration and redemption that comes from the Twelve. We might feel overwhelmed at the wreckage around us that we've tried so hard to live down or to which we may have surrendered in an attempt at peace.

God's message to us in the Minors is not to tear us down or to make us feel bad about our past choices. He means to clear the air and set forth a strong path forward with nothing hidden or making us stumble along the way as we follow Him in faith.

Over generations God's people had sunk into rebellion and corruption. God's ways were cast aside in favor of the ways of the world around them. The people of God had to endure the judgment of God in 586 B.C. when Jerusalem fell, the temple was destroyed, and God's people were carried into exile to a far away land. Looking around them at all the wreckage and ruin, they might have thought that there was no coming back from how far they had fallen and that God may have left them behind in their destruction with no hope of reconciliation.

We may have felt that way ourselves when having to come to terms with some choices we've made. The feeling of not knowing where to turn and that we have gone too far for God to forgive us may be a real feeling for many today. That's where our Minor Prophets shine the brightest. God always makes a way in His mercy and grace where there seems to be no way to return to Him.

FROM THE TWELVE

We can be so stubborn and prideful that judgment is the only thing that will break us so that we will listen to the God who wants only to forgive and restore. God can't be kicked out. He stays. Why? As crazy as it sounds given the way we can behave, He stays because He loves us. His judgment comes to break down all of the architecture of boasting and pride that clutters our lives and lands and keeps us from the redemption and restoration we long for.

(page 251)

A WORD FOR THOSE WHO HAD LOST EVERYTHING

OBADIAH c.585 - 500 B.C

Obadiah spoke most likely in about 585 B.C after the fall of Jerusalem and the Southern Kingdom to the Babylonians, and he had the right thing to say at the right time to some deeply

grieving people. Scholars disagree on when to date the book, but regardless of the date, the message was to encourage those who felt God had forgotten them. Obadiah spoke after a time of terrible conflict between God's people and their own neighbors, the people of Edom. What's worse is that the people of Edom were cousins to God's people, the Israelites. It was a long and bitter hatred that was nurtured over generations that resulted in the tragic cruelties that Obadiah was called to speak against. God showed through this mighty prophet that He was not only going to bring judgment against those who had acted in such cruelty against His people, He had not forgotten His once rebellious people and promised to lift them up and restore them to a marvelous kingdom of His own design.

Let's try to paint the picture. Imagine a spot in the center of ancient Jerusalem that is surrounded by rubble, filth, and charred beams that were once homes and marketplaces now lying in shattered bits all around. Smoke drifts about in the silent breeze rising from the smoldering piles that used to be a fabulous city capped off with a gleaming temple of white and bronze on the highest point. That temple is a ruin now, burned and broken. A lone dog barks in the distance, lost somewhere in an alleyway filled with wreckage. The remaining few people who survived the brutal attack by the most powerful army on earth stagger into the city center over the ruins, dodging the bodies trapped among the refuse. They say nothing. Some fall to the ground and weep. Hope is lost. God had poured out His wrath and abandoned them. . . or so they might think.

Then, from among the people rises a bearded and robed figure that raises his eyes above the rubble to the clear sky above. Lifting a hand he points his face in the direction of Edom and utters these words in full voice:

> Thus says the Lord God concerning Edom.
> (Obadiah 1)

God had not fallen silent. He had not forgotten His people, and He had seen all that had happened. He was rising up on behalf of

His people. He is not aloof and distant in our hardship, even in the hardship we earned by our own actions. He is near if we will turn to Him in faith.

I know for me trying to look ahead at the good that can come out of a tough situation is not exactly easy. It's very natural to sit in a big stew of "bah humbugs" and misery. The cruelty and loveless action that happened in Obadiah's day by the people of Edom against the Judeans (their own cousins!) were not God's doing, but they did not happen without His knowing about it. The focus here shifted high above the rubble and far into the future. God said through Obadiah that things were about to change. The nations might not have known it yet, but God was up to something that included them as well. And His eye was on that very city that lay in ruins in Obadiah's day: Jerusalem. The temple would be rebuilt and serve as the anchor for God's people until the parables of His own Son echoed through its courtyards over 500 years later. Still, it may have seemed all but impossible for the people in Obadiah's day to see through their own tears. God's view is a longer view than our own. It's an eternal view. It's a Kingdom view. He is working on things we can't quite see yet. Through the prophets, He helps us see as He sees.

Obadiah ended his book by saying that the Promised Land lost to the invading peoples would be reclaimed and that Jerusalem would once again be populated by "deliverers" brought there by God (Obadiah 21). God saw a time when His people would no longer be in the state that they were in during Obadiah's day. They would fill that mountain and would rule from there in God's Kingdom, and the kingdom established there would be God's alone. What must that have sounded like to the people who looked around and only saw devastation and ruin? Did it sound crazy? Did they laugh? Was their present situation just too much to bear? Or did they find hope in the words of a sovereign God who keeps His promises and had rescued them and delivered them countless times in the past?

It might be hard for us as Christians today to get fired up about Obadiah since the church worldwide as the body of Christ not defined by an earthly geography. Obadiah kind of seemed focused on land lost in war being returned and the bad folks getting what was coming to them. But if I see this book in the light of the whole Bible and see how God was working towards the Messiah, maybe it's not so foreign. God was preserving the old covenant and all of its promises until the day of the new covenant in Christ Jesus came to pass. **Obadiah is a reminder that God keeps His promises, that He does not reward evil, and that He is always about His greater Kingdom, built on the cornerstone of Jesus Christ.** Obadiah is part of God's greater redemptive story that is about restoring a right relationship with Him. That restoration is always done His way, not our way. His way is always better. He is faithful when we can be so faithless. He is a promise keeper when we can forget our promises and follow after things that hurt us. He is able to bring about His will no matter the situation. God knows how hard this world marred by sin can be. But He, in His goodness, does not forget those who are His by faith and call on His name in their distress and need. Lift your eyes above the rubble and smoke as Obadiah did. God is near through Christ His Son.

Have you seen God redeem and restore an area of your life or maybe a broken relationship by His work in you through Jesus? If so, what was it?

SEEK ME AND LIVE

 Read Amos 5:1-15 in your Bible.

In chapter 5 of Amos God said, "Hear now the words that I take up over you in lamentation, O house of Israel" (Amos 5:1). It was a lament that God spoke over them. Just like Hosea and like the Minor Prophets as a whole, He was utterly broken hearted over the awful things people could do to each other and to Him. The whirlwind of sin is a destroyer. God warned them harshly of this fact. But in the midst of these words of doom and judgment, God did it again. He showed His true heart: "Seek me and live" (Amos 5:4). And not just once: three times! "Seek the Lord and live" (Amos 5:6) and "Seek good and not evil that you may live" (Amos 5:14). Is it clear enough what He wants? Seek Him and live. "Hate evil and love good, and establish justice in the gate" (Amos 5:15). The gate of the city is where court was held and where people sought justice and fairness according to the good Law of God. Following God's way meant to hate evil and love good. His people were doing the exact opposite. God doesn't just let that ride. His words were strong here in Amos, but the loving heart of a good Father shines through. I hope you see that.

Sadly, it appears that the larger response to the words of God in Amos were total rejection. On the timeline of history, Amos spoke to the Northern Kingdom a few decades before the bitter prophesies he was called to proclaim came to pass. The people did not seek God. In fact, "The more they were called, the more they went astray" (Hosea 11:2). The end came as God said it would since nothing changed. 2 Kings recorded these heartbreaking words:

> In the ninth year of Hoshea, the king of Assyria captured Samaria... And this occurred because the people of Israel had sinned against the Lord their God who had brought them up out of the land of Egypt from under the hand of Pharaoh king of Egypt, and had feared other gods and walked in the customs of the nations whom the Lord drove out before the people of Israel and in the customs that the kings of Israel had practiced.
>
> (2 Kings 17:7-8)

> They abandoned all the commandments of the Lord their God, and made for themselves metal images of two calves; and they made an Asherah and worshiped all the host of

heaven and served Baal. And they burned their sons and their daughters as offerings and used divination and omens and sold themselves to do evil in the sight of the Lord, provoking Him to anger. Therefore the Lord was very angry with Israel and removed them out of His sight. None was left but the tribe of Judah only.

(2 Kings 17:16-18)

Awful. So if we ask the question, "Is there a limit to what God will take?" it seems the answer is "yes" in Amos' case. Now that Christ has come and the work of the cross is complete, the loss of salvation is not a fear for the Believer, but the strong discipline of God can not only be a possibility, it can be expected. God surely feels the same way about sin now as He did then. At the end of all things when Christ returns to claim His own who have trusted Him, the wrath of God stored up against the evil of mankind will be poured out in full on those who, like those of Amos' day, turned a deaf ear to God in favor of all their sin could devour. And God will likewise be heartbroken on that day of wrath over those who reaped His holy judgment. How bitter that must be for Him knowing that He created us all because it pleased His heart to no end to do so.

Without an honest and heartfelt response by His people in the Northern Kingdom that came from a deeply repentant heart for the generational evil they had done, the judgment would be inescapable.

'If they dig into [the depths of the grave]
   from there shall my hand take them,
if they climb up to heaven,
   from there will I bring them down,
Behold, the eyes of the Lord are
    upon the sinful kingdom,
  and I will destroy it from the surface
   of the ground,
except that I will not utterly destroy
  the house of Jacob,'

declares the Lord.

(Amos 9:2,8)

These are truly sobering words. Let them drive you to Him who is waiting to lavish His love and grace on any heart that is turned toward Him in honest confession. Remember how He reveals His character! "Seek Me and live." Look at what God said in Ezekiel about His deep desire to forgive instead of judge:

> Have I any pleasure in the death of the wicked, declares the Lord God, and not rather that he should turn from his way and live?
>
> (Ezekiel 18:23)

> Repent and turn from all your transgressions, lest iniquity be your ruin. Cast away from you all the transgressions that you have committed, and make yourselves a new heart and a new spirit! Why will you die, O house of Israel? For I have no pleasure in the death of anyone, declares the Lord God; so turn, and live.
>
> (Ezekiel 18:30-32)

"For I have no pleasure in the death of anyone," said God. The words and judgments in Amos were severe and sobering, but to His people God surely said, "Seek Me and live." And He meant it. In Christ now the same is true. "Take your burden to the Lord and leave it there," says the old hymn. God revealed His good and merciful character perfectly in Jesus, the Lamb of God who takes away the sins of the world (John 1:29). The Twelve help me to understand sin the way God does so that I don't play with it; I repent of it.

- What does it mean to you that God has no pleasure in the death of anyone, but rather that He calls us to return to Him in faith to bless us and save us in Christ? What does this say to you about God?

The very end of Amos takes a turn into brighter skies with a hopeful hue. In these last verses God revealed His true heart and desire for His people who come to Him now through Christ Jesus in faith believing. The promise is still true.

> "Behold, the days are coming" declares
>   the Lord,
> "when the plowman shall overtake the
>   reaper
> and the treader of grapes him who
>   sows the seed...
>
> I will restore the fortunes of my people Israel."
>   (Amos 9:13,14)

God told His people about a day that He had planned when the abundance would be so great for His people that they would barely be able to keep up with it all. He would restore their fortunes Himself, as in Joel when He promised to restore the years that the locusts had eaten. I can say for myself, that often the goodness of God overwhelms me, and it's hard not to be moved to tears. I can be so stubborn, so thankless, so hard–headed, and stiff-necked that His mercy shown to me which I do not deserve stops me in my tracks. The gentle breath of His Holy Spirit reminds me of the way

I should take. Sometimes in those moments I get down on my face in prayer but have nothing to say that could match the feeling of His grace. Again, I ask like the Psalmist in Scripture, "What is man that you are mindful of him, the son of man that you care for him?" (Psalm 8:4) He doesn't *have* to restore anything. He would be right and just to leave us rebellious folk to the darkness of our hearts and the wreckage we make of our lives. But He doesn't. In Christ He calls to us one and all, no matter where we've been or how far we've gone, to return to Him so that He can restore us to Himself. He is no friend to sin. "Friendship with the world is enmity towards God," James reminded us in his letter (James 4:4). You do not want to be an enemy of God. He does not sit by while sin destroys. And when He acts, it is definite. You do not want to be a friend to sin. Sin will leave you in ruins. The great furnace that is the book of Amos is about as clear and direct as you can get on these two points. Being a friend to God and an enemy of the dominion of sin is the way to go. In Amos the good and consistent character of God shines through. Why does He call out to us and warn us? Why does He love us? I don't know. But He does love us. He truly is a wonderful God.

THE WAY OUT

Without Hosea chapter 14, it might be one of the saddest books we could read. But God does not lead us to the valley of the shadow of death; He leads us *through* it. I can say that for me personally just writing this little portion of my thoughts on walking with the Twelve has been intensely introspective. So much of my own failures, stubbornness, insecurities, and feelings of unworthiness have been laid bare before God. Each time I go through these great books and spend time with these guys, they hone and sharpen my spirit in new ways. That's why I love them so much. So when I stop squirming and making excuses and I finally open my wounded heart up to God, He then provides something desperately needed—a way out, a way to return to Him.

The very first word in Hosea's last chapter could be the one word that sums up the entire book. It's not an easy word, but did you expect an easy word from this guy? Best translated, the word is "Repent." The English Standard Version that I use says, "Return," but the idea is one of repentance—to stop going in the direction we're going and turn fully to God. I have found in my own life that repentance is the beginning of any significant transformation in Christ—certainly at the first confession of faith in Him, but also in times when we know we've strayed and need to return. We can't take the chains with us that separate us from Him when we do return. It doesn't work that way. We have to get real and "lay aside every weight and sin which clings so closely " (Hebrews 12:1).

- Why do you think it can seem easier to us to keep things status quo and live with our sinful patterns rather than take them to God through Christ to change us and lead us in new paths apart from those old patterns?

If God were to bring the might of Hosea's words to us and then provide no way to return or to be redeemed, that would be terrible. Have you ever had someone call out all your flaws and failures just to watch you squirm? That's not what God does. Ever. He is a redeeming God, full of compassion and mercy. So let's be very thankful for chapter 14! This one is packed like a Snickers bar. Hosea has truly left the best for last.

Return, O Israel, to the Lord your

God,
for you have stumbled because of
your iniquity.
Take with you words
and return to the Lord."

(Hosea 14:1-2)

I'm a little overwhelmed at the goodness of God here. He does
not leave it up to us to find Him. It's not up to us to discover some
secret door or do battle with the cosmos to return to God. He has
done all the work and sets the path right before us. "Take with you
words," He said. He even gives us the words to say, not as some
magic charm or a rambling and repetitive mantra, but as a heartfelt
prayer. In 1 John 1:9 we see this gift come to its fullest realization in
Christ, that if we "confess our sins, He is faithful and just to forgive
us and cleanse us of all unrighteousness." Look at what God asked
here through Hosea:

Say to Him,
  'Take away all iniquity;
accept what is good,
  and we will pay with bulls
  the vows of our lips.
Assyria shall not save us,
  We will not ride on horses
And we will say no more, "Our God,"
  To the work of our hands,
For in you the orphan finds mercy.

(Hosea 14:2-3)

Hosea has his own style, so some of this wording is difficult. In
short he is telling us to pray earnestly to God to do what only He
can do: take away the stain and ugliness of our sin before Him. We
are to ask God through Christ to accept the good and heartfelt
prayer from our lips that is better than any religious sacrifice
because we confess our utter dependence on Him. He said to
confess that we have turned to powerful institutions and people

to save us, or even worse, to our own might and self-reliance. We have made gods out of our own work and desired to control good and evil in our lives by our own strength and intelligence. We are truly as needy as orphans with no protector, and we plead for God's mercy. "Bring these words to me," God says, "and let me heal you." How beautiful. **These words cut right to heart of our rebellion and selfishness. These words strip away the fake stuff and leave us bare before the God we have so deeply offended. But He gives us the words. He shows us the path. He lights the way out. Confess and return.**

The broken family picture that Hosea opened with in describing the breakdown between God and His people is redeemed in the last chapter. When we get real with God through Christ Jesus "in whom we have redemption, the forgiveness of sins" (Colossians 1:14), the redemption and restoration God desires is ours as well. How does God respond to the prayer offered in humility and repentant faith? Does He leave us in a puddle of tears on the floor wondering if we'll ever be good enough? No. Look at how God responded:

> I will heal their apostasy;
>   I will love them freely,
>   for my anger has turned from them.
> I will be like the dew to Israel,
>   he shall blossom like the lily;
>   he shall take root like the trees of
>   Lebanon;
>
> They shall return and dwell beneath my
>   shadow;
>   they shall flourish like the grain,
> they shall blossom like the vine.
>   (Hosea 14:4-5,7)

This is the heart of God on display. "I will heal their apostasy; I will love them freely." Get real with God. Take with you words of

157

deepest confession. Lay your sin and burdens down before Christ our Redeemer and Sustainer, God's Son, sent not to condemn the world but to save the world through Him (John 3:17). God is the faithful husband in Hosea's family picture. He loves you more deeply than you can fully know.

CONCLUSION AND TAKEAWAYS

There may be things in our past or even current trials that make us fearful of being open and real with God. But those things close us off from freedom in Christ and keep us trapped in patterns of thoughts and action that hurt us. God shows us the way out. That way is one where we have to leave those burdens behind that keep us from walking in close fellowship with Him and with our brothers and sisters in Christ. In Christ today, we can lift our eyes from wreckage all around us and follow the good paths set forward by God through our mighty Minors who looked forward to Jesus' redeeming work and love beyond bounds poured out for us on His cross. Don't play with sin; repent of it. Freedom and peace are yours today through Jesus our living hope!

- What are your takeaways from this study? What made the most impact for you?

- What are next steps God is leading you toward in walking through those things with Him? What may need to change for you? What conversations might you need to have with someone about these things?

WEEK

WALK THE TALK
TOUGH AS A MINOR PROPHET

Well, we've made it to the final week! I hope you've enjoyed exploring some of the major themes in the Minor Prophets. Spending time with them forces us to ask tough questions of ourselves and be open and real with God about areas of our walk of faith in Christ that may need His cultivating work in order to better produce good fruit. It's always a good thing to come close to God and let Him work deeply within us, even if that process can feel like we're sitting in a furnace. "Uncomfortable" does not always equal "bad." Once the work is done and insights from it are gained, God raises us up to stronger faith in Christ by His Spirit to look without fear into the future and to stand boldly as beloved sons and daughters by faith. **What can be said of our mighty Minors is this: when times were at their worst, these guys were at their best.** No matter where we may be at present in our walk with Christ, time spent with the Minor Prophets is fruitful and encouraging.

Let's look at three things that stand out as strong character qualities that these men of God seemed to share that gave them the guts and grit they needed to speak His truth to a world determined to oppose it.

WELCOMING THE FURNACE WORK OF GOD

James the Apostle knew something about the furnace of God and the good work He does there to prepare us for vibrant Christian life. In fact, James opened his New Testament letter with this statement:

> Count it all joy, my brothers, when you meet trials of various kinds, for you know that the testing of your faith produces steadfastness. And let steadfastness have its full effect, that you may be perfect and complete, lacking nothing.
> (James 1:2-4)

The phrase "testing of your faith" comes from the Greek word *dokimos* and relates to the firing process a pot must go through before it is ready for use. The clay is shaped by the potter and then placed into a blazing hot kiln to harden. In James' day, if that pot made it through the firing process without cracking, the word *"dokimos"* was written on the bottom of it by the potter. That was proof that this pot made it through the fire and didn't break up. It was ready for anything that it was required for. James was talking here about the kind of fire found in the furnace of God. The "testing of our faith" can come through persecution by the world because we follow Jesus. It can also be from personal trials or hardships. They can be part of His furnace. But just because times are hard or because people are cruel doesn't always mean that's His furnace. Surely God works all things for our good, but the furnace of God is different. The potter shapes the pot and then places it in the fire himself. God uses His furnace the same way—it isn't just to test us: it's to transform us by His own work and His own fire.

According to James, the end goal of God's furnace is steadfast faith in Him, full and lacking nothing. The furnace of God *produces* steadfast faith. That's why it's different: it has a purpose. Too many Christians, I believe, won't stay in the furnace when God turns up the heat to burn off the impurity and weakness within the vessel. Like "rend your hearts and not your garments" in Joel, the furnace of God can be a deeply painful place, especially for the prideful and rebellious. It gets too hot, and we hop out back into the lives we used to live that made us weak in our faith and impure in our minds. In doing so we render ourselves unfit for the greater use that was ours if we had stayed with God and let Him do His refining work. The furnace of God often feels like suffering because we aren't satisfying our lusts, pleasing our flesh, stroking our egos, or catering to our prideful expectations. We are there in the fire utterly dependent upon God and often covered in heartfelt tears. It's not about simply surviving. The furnace is about producing something that wasn't there before: *steadfast* faith in God. It will not be available without the intense heat of God's purifying hand shaping us and creating it within us.

It's not hard to spot the men and women with a steadfast faith formed deep within them by opening up their whole life to the intense work of God. They have a Minor Prophet fire in them. They're not always tough looking on the outside like some poser. They're tough on the inside.

People who have allowed God to do His work in them the ones you can rely on to go right into the ring for you in prayer to do battle with the Devil himself because they have no fear of his accusations compared to Christ's redeeming power. They are defined by an unshakable faith in God Almighty and in the risen Jesus who defeated sin, death, and Hell triumphing over them by His cross (Colossians 2:15). Nothing can hold those sons and daughters of God. There are far too few believers in Christ who have welcomed the furnace of God in their lives, whereas many more limp by day after day shackled by sin and hounded by Hell. The Minor Prophets can be an introduction to this kind of refining fire if we will be open to God's heat on the things we know need to be burned out of our lives to make us ready for all He has for us in Christ.

Living like a Minor Prophet, as it were, can be summed up in three words: *confidence in God*. That means trusting confidently in God Almighty no matter what is going on in the world around us. There is nothing that the devil can throw at us to take away what

God has given through faith in Christ: hope, determination of mission, and the life-giving knowledge that He will never leave us or forsake us but works all things for the good of those who love God and are called according to His purpose (Romans 8:28). It is One who walked upon the waves that we follow. What would threaten to take us out was no threat to Him. In Christ, we can walk in confidence knowing that though we may have trouble in this world, He has overcome the world. It is the tested faith that can boldly proclaim such things.

- Have you had a time when your faith was sorely tested? Are you in that time now? How did walking through that time with the Lord shape your faith? What can you share now with others that you could not share before that time?

- What is the most challenging part of yielding to God's work in your life? Do you sometimes close areas of your life off to God's good work?

I SHALL RISE

One of the biggest challenges in times of trial and hardship is keeping a right perspective. An eternal perspective is one that looks above the wreckage and rumbling going on around us to consider the ebb and flow of human activity according to God's ways and work in the world instead of our own limited view. It requires us to trust Him.

The last chapter of Micah is a real triumph of faith, but it began with Micah's looking around with his prophetic eyes to see the destruction that was coming because of the persistent sins of God's people. Micah likened the feeling of living in that day to the hard disappointment of a poor harvest when the outlook for the whole year was compromised due to hunger and poverty to come. The people who follow after God were nowhere to be found. There was a famine of faith in the land. Micah said:

> The godly has perished from the earth,
>   and there is no one upright among
>   mankind:
> They all lie in wait for blood,
>   and each hunts the other with a net.
>
> The best of them is like a brier,
>   the most upright of them a thorn
>   hedge.
>
> The day of your watchmen, of your
>   punishment, has come.
>   (Micah 7:2,4)

It was actually dangerous to live among these people. Micah described the days to come as a picture of family and community breakdown. It would be a total collapse from the inside with no one to trust for help: "A man's enemies are the men of his own house" (Micah 7:6). They couldn't trust their spouse, their kids, their friends, their neighbors—no one. Everyone had collapsed upon the sinful self. That sounds terrible. Jesus said in Matthew 12:25, "Every kingdom divided against itself is laid waste, and no city or house divided against itself will stand." The Southern Kingdom had become completely unstable. The societal foundations were crumbling and the judgment of God was at hand. But Micah shifted his prophetic gaze in another direction and did so with a confident smile. He was not worried for himself or for the faithful remnant that would remain by God's grace. How is that possible in light of the judgment he knew was coming?

One word: relationship. Micah walked with God and knew Him through a personal relationship by faith. That changed everything. In the midst of it all knowing that he would have to live through the wrath of God that was coming on the land, Micah said:

> But as for me, I will look to the Lord;
> I will wait for the God of my salvation;
> my God will hear me.
>
> (Micah 7:7)

Micah said plainly, "I'm not sure what you all are going to do when the bottom drops out and there is no place to hide, but as for me, I'm not seeing things the way you are. My eyes are not looking to the world around me. I will wait confidently for my God who will hear me and save me according to His steadfast love." Wow. Those three words: "I will wait." Without complete trust in God on every level, those words are hard. Micah's unshakable faith in the God of his salvation did not come by accident. It was not a disregard for reality or a pie-in-the-sky mentality that he had. It was a deep-seated confidence in the character of God because Micah knew His character through a personal walk with Him. That is the difference. The hope of Micah was not based on his own work or on the conditions of the world around him. He did not run from God when things got difficult before, and he won't run now—not because Micah was a great man. It's only because God is a great God who hears and saves. Micah's kind of hope comes through fire and faith, through testing and perseverance with God's help. Hope like that does not disappoint or put us to shame (Romans 5:5). Staring down the throat of tragic events to come that God revealed to Micah, our amazing prophet said boldly:

> Rejoice not over me, my enemy;
>> When I fall I shall rise;
> When I sit in darkness,
>> The Lord will be a light to me.
>>>> (Micah 7:8)

Wow. What an amazing expression of faith in God.

It can be so hard to trust God like that when things get rough. We use phrases like "staying positive" or "choosing the good" to talk about how we are surviving hard times. But I don't think that's the same thing as trust. The "valley of the shadow of death" is real. Our response to God while walking through it should be just as real. To "fear no evil because God is with us" (Psalm 23) is not choosing the good—it is putting our trust in God who alone can make the difference. It is a bold response in times when fear can be all around. To trust in God in dark days is a strong genuine response for followers of Christ no matter the situation.

Living like a Minor Prophet requires something else besides welcoming God's work in their lives: it requires *God's higher perspective*. Micah did not run from God in times of great trial. He ran to God. When what we have done shatters the foundations of our lives and family and when there is nowhere else to go but to God, we can still be tempted to run from Him. We can sense the ruin that is coming somehow and can stare right into the face of bitter consequence and *still* not bow the knee in confessing our brokenness before God. "I will bear it," says Micah, because in God's transforming grace, "When I fall I shall rise." He trusted in God to raise him up.

He will bring me out into the light;
I shall look upon his vindication.

(Micah 7:9)

The times didn't have to be good for Micah to praise God and faithfully serve Him. That is worth repeating. He did that because he knew and had experienced God's character in his life *personally*.

- Has there been a time in your life when you didn't know who to trust and you felt that if you shared your heart on a matter that people might be hostile to your deeply held belief? What was your response to that situation?

- What is the hardest part of trusting God in fearful times or in times where the outcome is unclear at the moment? How does trusting in God's character help you to look at the future differently? What part of His character do you cling to most?

FOUR WORDS YOU WANT TO HEAR

Lastly, in addition to welcoming God's work in our lives and letting God give us a right perspective, we need one more thing to be Minor Prophet tough. In fact, without this one thing, none of the rest can happen. Throughout the Bible men and women of faith were able to lean their full spiritual weight on this one thing even if all else seemed to be crumbling around them at the time: His presence. **Living like a Minor Prophet with an unshakable faith is only possible because, through Christ our Redeemer, God is with us.** If God is in the work, there is nothing all the powers of evil can do to stop it.

If you remember in the Minor Prophet Haggai's day, the job the returned exiles were called by God to do was being squashed by enemies of that work all around them. They wanted to give up, but Haggai said to get up and get to work! God had given them a history-shaping job to do in rebuilding the temple. He had not given up on working in and through them to bring about His will.

"All of that sounds great, but the work is still difficult. It is still opposed at every turn. We are still afraid. We know the house of God needs to be rebuilt, but can't you do something about making things easier for us?" the people might have said. Sometimes the response needs to happen whether conditions change or not. Sometimes we need to strengthen our hands in the face of opposition to what God is doing and set about doing the work He's given us anyway. That's exactly what the leadership and the people of Haggai's day did in response to these words from God.

At the very beginning of this short book, Haggai mentioned the two people God addressed with His message. Zerubbabel was appointed by the king of Persia to head the rebuilding effort and answer directly to him. Joshua (or Jeshua) was the high priest in charge of making sure the aspects and duties of the temple service were observed properly according to the Law of Moses. Both the civic and religious leadership were the ones God was focusing on in His message in Haggai.

Discouragement runs down hill. If the leadership is sucking wind, the people underneath them will reflect the insecure messaging and attitude of leadership. If the leadership is afraid, the people won't be inspired by them to work boldly or with courage on any initiative. But if the leadership is bold in its vision, strong and courageous in its efforts, the people will respond. Haggai was sent to the struggling leadership to give this bold vision. And the leadership responded.

They didn't throw up a bunch of excuses. Haggai recorded, "And the people feared the Lord" (Haggai 1:12). They obeyed and got up to do what God called them to do. What sustained the effort? What gave them confidence to start again? Four words did:

> Then Haggai, the messenger of the Lord, spoke to the people with the Lord's message. "I am with you, declares the Lord."
>
> (Haggai 1:13)

There it is: "I am with you." Those four words erased the fear, doubt, discouragement, and lethargy. "Don't worry about what the people of the land will say or do. I am with you," God seemed to say. Those powerful words are all that are needed even today to inspire Christian leadership and fuel the people of God to do bold and courageous work for the sake of the Gospel. We do the work because *God is with us* in the work. It reminds me of the time when Peter and John were arrested by the annoyed religious leaders of their day for teaching in Jesus' name and proclaiming His resurrection. They both got the shakedown from that leadership and were charged to never speak in Jesus' name ever again. How did they respond?

> But Peter and John answered them, "Whether it is right in the sight of God to listen to you rather than to God, you

must judge, for we cannot but speak of what we have seen
and heard."

(Acts 4:19)

You know what fired those guys up? They knew that God was *with*
them through the Spirit at work *within* them. That confidence
urged them on. They feared no man. Through the work of the
Holy Spirit, miracles were being done in Jesus' name and many
were coming to faith every day. The threats and oppression of the
misguided religious leaders did not carry the crippling weight that
could silence them. Why not? God was with them—encouraging
them, working through them, filling their mouths with the Gospel,
and leading them in each step. Was it easy? Nope. They were just
arrested and threatened. Harsher times were coming for the church.
Did that stop them? No way. They had work to do that God had
given them. Guess what? You and I have work to do in our homes
and community for the sake of the Gospel. Depending on where
you are in the world, this work can be strongly opposed by many
holding power. But without disrespecting those in authority,
working for the Gospel of peace so that all can hear it must
continue. God is with us through Christ our Lord. In compassion,
prayer, boldness, and with courage, do the work. Haggai shows us
how. Never forget that God empowers the work He calls us to do.
He is with us.

- Near the end of the incredible chapter 8 of the book of
  Romans, the Apostle Paul declared this statement in response
  to the mighty work of God's salvation though Christ: "If God
  be for us, who can be against us?" (Romans 8:31). What does
  the knowledge of God's presence in every season of life as a
  follower of Christ mean to you?

CONCLUSION AND TAKEAWAYS

Welcoming God's work in our lives, maintaining a God-given perspective by faith, and leaning on the truth that God is with us who trust in Christ His Son are three major themes that can give us the confidence in God that the Minor Prophets had during the difficult days that they faced.

- What are your takeaways from this study? What made the most impact for you?

- What are next steps God is leading you toward in walking with more confident faith in Him? What may need to change for you? What conversations could you have with someone struggling with trusting God?

NOTES

INTRODUCTORY CHAPTER

All Biblical quotes used in this book are taken from the English Standard Version unless otherwise noted.

WEEK ONE

1. C.S. Lewis, Mere Christianity (New York, NY: Touchstone Simon & Schuster, 1943, 1945, 1952, renewed 1980) 24

2. W. Elwell and B. Beltzel, "Righteousness" Baker Encyclopedia of the Bible (Grand Rapids, MI: Baker Book House, 1988) 1860-1862

3. A. Heschel, The Prophets (Peabody, MA: Hendrickson, 1962) 201

4. From a personal text converstation with friend J Bagge December 2020

5. A. Heschel, The Prophets (Peabody, MA: Hendrickson, 1962) 200

6. A. Rogers, Love Worth Finding radio program from Bellevue Baptist Church, Memphis, TN heard by me in July 2017

WEEK TWO

1. Thomas Cranmer was a leader of the English Reformation in the 1500s A.D. during the reign of Henry VIII and was a highly influential voice of Christian thought and practice.

WEEK THREE

1. T. McComiskey, The Minor Prophets Volume Three (Grand Rapids, MI: Baker Academic, 1998) 97
2. A.W. Tozer, Knowledge of the Holy (New York, NY: Harper Collins, 1992) 10

WEEK FOUR

1. K. Barker and W. Bailey, Zephaniah New American Commentary (Nashville, TN: Broadman and Holman, 1997) 434-435

WEEK FIVE

1. J. Calvin, "the human heart is a perpetual idol factory" Institutes (Louisville, KY: Westminster John Knox Press, 1960) 108
2. S. and J. Berenstain, Inside Outside Upside Down (New York, NY Random House, 1968,1997)
3. Doctor Zhivago (Metro-Goldwyn Mayer, 1965)

TIME LINE OF MINOR PROPHETS

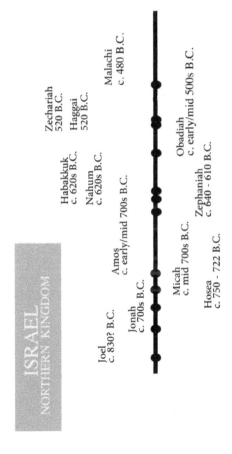

ISRAEL
NORTHERN KINGDOM

JUDAH
SOUTHERN KINGDOM

Joel
c. 830? B.C.

Jonah
c. 700s B.C.

Amos
c. early/mid 700s B.C.

Habakkuk
c. 620s B.C.

Nahum
c. 620s B.C.

Zechariah
520 B.C.

Haggai
520 B.C.

Malachi
c. 480 B.C.

Micah
c. mid 700s B.C.

Hosea
c. 750 - 722 B.C.

Zephaniah
c. 640 - 610 B.C.

Obadiah
c. early/mid 500s B.C.

ABOUT THE AUTHOR

Parker Bradley is passionate about encouraging deeper Biblical understanding for lay leaders and Bible Study teachers in the local church. As a lay leader and teacher, he writes to open up challenging passages of Scripture for Bible studies to easily engage. As a video producer he has traveled to many parts of the world working with churches, artists, and Christian ministries to help tell their stories to others. He earned a Masters from Regent University and resides near Nashville, Tennessee.

CPSIA information can be obtained
at www.ICGtesting.com
Printed in the USA
BVHW092247110621
609354BV00006B/1590

9 781638 775768